DEAR
MEM FOX,
I have read all your books
even the pathetic ones

BY THE SAME AUTHOR

Possum Magic

Wilfrid Gordon McDonald Partridge

Teaching Drama to Young Children

Hattie and the Fox

A Cat Called Kite

Guess What?

Koala Lou

With Love, at Christmas

Night Noises

Shoes from Grandpa

Radical Reflections: Passionate Opinions on Teaching, Learning, and Living

Time for Bed

DEAR
MEM FOX,

I have read all your books even the pathetic ones

and other incidents in the life of a children's book author

by Mem Fox

A HARVEST ORIGINAL
HARCOURT BRACE & COMPANY
San Diego   New York   London

Library of Congress Cataloging-in-Publication Data
Fox, Mem, 1946–
[Mem's the word]
Dear Mem Fox, I have read all your books
even the pathetic ones: and other incidents in the
life of a children's book author/Mem Fox.
— 1st Harvest ed.
p.   cm.
Originally published: Mem's the word.
Ringwood, Vic.: Penguin Books Australia, 1990.
"A Harvest original."
ISBN 0-15-658676-2
1. Fox, Mem, 1946– —Biography.   2. Authors,
Australian—20th century—Biography.   3. Children's
stories—Authorship.   I. Title.
PR9619.3.F66Z467   1992
823—dc20   91-58713

Designed by Trina Stahl

Printed in the United States of America

First Harvest edition 1992
I H G F E D

For Felicity who started it all

For Tom who found Julie

For Julie who found magic

For John who found Omnibus

For Omnibus who found me

And for Malcolm, who's always there.

Contents

Contents

DEAR
MEM FOX,
I have read all your books
even the pathetic ones

Introduction

Distinguished readers, ladies and gentlemen, girls and boys, it gives me great pleasure to introduce my autobiography, written after my youth and before my old age.

You may be wondering why I have written it now, rather than later, so I will tell you. I had cancer once, but survived—obviously. Since then life has become more precious, more urgent, and possibly more temporary. I have told my story now in case there is no "later."

I have other reasons, also, for having put pen to paper at this time, but they are woven into the fabric of these pages and will be revealed as the story unfolds.

Let me begin by saying . . .

1

Once Upon a Time

Once upon a time, and it's a true story this time, two Huguenot families fled persecution in France and settled in England. The name of the first was Devereux, and the name of the second, Perdriau. The Devereux family anglicized its name to Duesbury. Descendants of both these families settled eventually, and respectably—that is to say, they were *not* convicts—in Australia.

Effie Duesbury, my great-aunt on my mother's side, lived for a time in Kissing Point Road, Turramurra, New South Wales. Her age and spinsterhood and the incongruity of her address attracted me much as a heroine might on the first pages of a nineteenth-century novel. Who was she? Who was I? When I was fifteen and feeling rootless as an Australian child in Africa, longing to belong, I wrote to her. "Tell me the story of us," I asked.

The tale she told was filled with Methodist preachers and speakers of great eloquence; with the founders of the famous Crown Derby china works in England; with naval officers and judges in the early colonization of Australia; with the man who started the first ferry service across Sydney Harbor, a hundred years before the famous bridge was built; with writers of journals and writers of letters; with teachers and storytellers; and even with a great-grandmother who, it seems, laughed as often and as loudly as I do.

Until I reread Auntie Eff's letter I had thought that I was somehow *vastly* original. I was mistaken. My writing and teaching, my storytelling and speaking, my journal- and letter-writing were all present in my past. Frankly, I found this a little disappointing. How much more fascinating it would have been had I turned out to have been a belly dancer, a combat pilot, or a Carmelite nun. Instead I am merely the latest figure to be cut from the same old pattern that has been lying around in my family for generations.

My mother's father was one of many Methodist ministers among generations of Methodist ministers. My mother's mother graduated with a B.A. from Sydney University in 1908—a most unusual achievement for a woman at that time.

Both my parents' families were involved in politics and in the early feminist movement. Christabel Pankhurst, daughter of the well-known suffragette Emily, stayed with my maternal grandparents during a tour of Australia in 1927, which may account for the fact that my mother became and remains a much more fearsome feminist than I will ever be.

My mother was born in 1915 and christened Nancy Walkden Brown. She was the second of five children, the only girl among a tribe of brothers. I'm led to believe she was rather unconventional, never ladylike, but very bright. By the age of nineteen she, too, had a B.A. from Sydney University. She is still wild and unconventional. Consequently I never had the chance to become a lady—I wouldn't have dared to be such a disappointment.

In the late thirties, before the Second World War, this mother of mine became a teaching missionary in Rabaul, in Papua New Guinea. And after that, before she married my father, she married Ralph Fletcher, who was killed in 1942 fighting the Japanese in New Guinea. They had been married for less than a year. Then she met my father, but that story will have to wait for a moment since I have not yet introduced him.

On my father's side of the family there were also teachers and writers, political activists and early settlers. My great-great-grandfather Reuben Partridge arrived in Australia from England in 1839. At that time the population of the state of South Australia was so insignificant that his letters were addressed to "Mr. Partridge, South Australia."

My father's father was a journalist. My paternal grandmother was a radical trailblazer in Montessori education and left-wing politics. In the 1911 photograph of the delegates to the annual Labor (i.e., Democrat) Party conference, she is the only woman. As a woman in my family I've had a lot to live up to: sitting around and not doing much has never been an option.

5

My father, Wilfrid Gordon McDonald Partridge, was born in 1912. (Reveling in the happy rhythm of his name, I used it as the title of my second book.) "Partridge" gave rise to many a weak joke, especially at Christmas. My sister Jan, in London, has a pear tree in her garden and so do I. We can hardly stand it! The name Fox has been light relief in comparison.

My father went to an Important Private School that he detested. Nevertheless, he became a teacher at the school the year after he left, taken on by his alma mater to weather the times of the Great Depression. He had never intended to teach but found he had a gift for it. The school nurtured him and tolerated him although he was left-wing in his politics and a passionate advocate of pacifism—fifty years before *Feathers and Fools*, my own predictably pacifist book, appeared. He studied for his B.A. at Adelaide University, then reluctantly decided to become an education officer in the Air Force during the Second World War. After the war, and when I was a baby, he took up further study and typed the final copy of his M.A. thesis in the bathroom of Auntie Eff's house, the only place where my crying did not disturb him.

My parents met in 1935 at a national conference of the Student Christian Movement. Unlike the conservative charismatic Christians who abound among my present students, my parents were radical, intellectual, and political in their Christianity and remain so.

They married in 1945. As they drove to their honeymoon hideaway they discussed the philosophical problem of sex roles within a household: was cleaning the grate a man's job

or a woman's? The solution, as it turned out, was to live in
Africa and have someone else do it for them.

Their home at the time was in Melbourne, and it was
there that I was born on March 5, 1946. In October of that
year, deeply disappointed that living in China was politically
out of the question, we sailed off to Africa so that my parents
could live happily ever after being teaching missionaries in
the British colony of Southern Rhodesia. The boat to South
Africa took six weeks, and the train from Cape Town north
to Bulawayo, two and a half days. My diapers were washed
one by one in the tiny hand basin and held out of the windows
to dry. Black ash and smoke belched backwards from the
engine, speckling them with filth.

At last the journey ended. On Hope Fountain Mission
the jacaranda trees were in full bloom, a glorious blue, brave
in the white heat, bold above the red dust. Africa caught
my parents up and has never let them go.

2

Growing Up in Africa

In early January 1988 I went back to Africa, recaptured my past, and bottled its essences. The first essence was Hope Fountain, the mission I grew up on. It's eleven miles from the city of Bulawayo, where my parents now live, and there's a bitumen road nearly all the way. The bitumen stops abruptly at a cattle grid that marks the entrance. One Sunday, with my father, I went to church at Hope Fountain and as the car rattled down the stony hill towards our former house, memories of my childhood began to bounce around my head. I'd spent most of my first nineteen years in this place.

On either side of the road, green from good rains, were the thorn trees whose oozing gum is soft and clear and sweet to eat. Long white thorns, as sharp as arrows, cover their branches like awkward Christmas candles. As a kid I went barefoot and often got thorns in my feet. Whenever that happened, I'd limp to the nearest thorn tree and break off one of the long thorns before I squatted down in the bare red earth to poke the little thorn out with the big one. My feet remain tough—I can walk on gravel without flinching —but they're so wide from going barefoot as a child that they still protest and nag with pain when I coax them into shoes.

Beyond the thorn trees is the dam, one of the favorite places of my past. In the dry season the sun beat down, cracking the earth around the edges of the shrinking water. Carefully, we'd see who could lift the biggest saucer of curled dried mud without breaking it. In the rainy season we caught tadpoles and skimmed flat stones across the brown water, and the boys, crazy with bravery, rode their bikes across the dam wall even though it had disappeared under a torrent of water. The boys thought I was watching them, but I never was. My eyes were always squeezed tight against the danger. What if they'd slipped and fallen into the dam? Or worse, what if they'd toppled over the other side onto the rocks below?

The old football field looked the same. No grass, of course. The men students played football on hard red earth and still do. I learned to drive on the football field, taught by the sons of another of the missionaries. Round and round we'd cruise, in and out of the football posts, missing them by a whisker, speeding up and spinning around in perfect wheelies again and again, coughing with laughter in the clouds of dust.

Beside the football field is the bus stop. I detested the days when Mum couldn't pick me up and I'd have to take the bus instead. School was from 7:40 A.M. to 12:50 P.M., except on Wednesdays, when it went on till 4:00 P.M. The air in the bus was stifling, even though we whites sat at the front. Africans had to sit at the back. I knew with embarrassment that it was unjust to favor Europeans in this way, because my parents had told me so and anyway I felt it. I was sometimes all alone in the front when the back half of the bus was packed with hot people, fainting hens, and wilting produce from the markets. The steamy smells of sweat and chicken manure wafted into my domain, nauseating me with guilt, but it was the law and I had to accept it. If I'd tried to sit at the back, the driver, an African, would have stopped the bus and made a terrible fuss. I preferred the silent humiliation of sitting alone in the front because I was a child, not a revolutionary, in a racist country.

There used to be a thorn tree near the bus stop, where people would gather for meager shade. I heard unearthly sounds coming from there once—it was close to our house—so I leaped onto my bike and raced round to see what it was. A small crowd of Africans had gathered to watch a woman writhing at the base of the tree, to which she'd been tied with strips of cloth. White froth spat from her mouth as she moaned and screamed.

"What's happening?" I asked.

"Never mind, Merri," said one of my friends. "She's

having a fit. She's mad but she'll be all right soon. You better go home now."

I couldn't go home. I was transfixed.

Up past the grove of gum trees planted by my homesick father in 1946 is the first house we lived in. My parents boiled water to drink until I was two years old, then they saw me one day kneeling under the communal tap on the mission, drinking from it. Mum yelled and carried on, I remember, but the African kids laughed and told her I'd been doing it for ages. After all, it was just outside our gate, and easy to reach. The copper taste is still in my mouth as I write.

African women came from all over the mission to the tap to fill huge tin drums with water. They wound a cloth into a circle and placed it on their heads before they lifted those great drums of water onto the tops of their heads, slowly, steadily—hardly spilling a drop. Often they had babies strapped to their backs with blankets, but still they never spilled the water. Two or three women might come from the same village and as they walked home single file along a narrow path, backs straight and strong, heads and water held high, they sang in wonderful harmonies that still move me. African singing, in news bulletins or in films, especially the singing of the African national anthem, "Nkosi Sikelel' i Africa," plunges me into a well of nostalgia.

My Australian mother used to worry about many aspects of my growing up in Africa, although many of the dangers would have been just as immediate in Australia, especially on a farming property. Cattle sometimes got inside our fences and my mother once watched me, at eighteen months, walk directly under an ox. Snakes were another hazard. At the age of six I remember seeing a deadly puff adder weave its way between the wheels of my sister's pram, but I had the sense not to scream. Mum kept a crowbar by the back door specifically for snakes. The puff adder was a greeny-gray pulp by the time she'd finished with it.

She used to be anxious about my being strapped to the back of our house girl, Dorla, but Dorla told her not to worry: "It's African custom, Mrs. Partridge." I never fell off and I never cried: the rhythm of Dorla's movements kept me contented and calm. When I was older, I used to try to strap dolls onto my own back, but they always fell off. I still can't work out how African women manage it and make it safe.

As I grew up I became fluent in Ndebele, the local African language, because my friends were all children of the Amandebele tribe. ("Matabele" is another name for the same people.) I used to annoy Mum by giving her cheek in Ndebele, which she couldn't understand, and she'd have to shrug her shoulders and say to the house girl, "What did she say, the little monkey?"

From that first house Dorla and I used to watch the Hope Fountain students going down the hill from their classrooms to their dormitories at the end of the day.

"Who's that one?" I'd ask.

"That's Ida Thebe," Dorla would reply.

"What does *Thebe* mean?"

"Mat."

"Hello, Miss Mat!" I'd yell out.

"And who's that?"

"Olipah Ngwenya."

"What's *Ngwenya?*"

"Crocodile."

"Hello, Miss Crocodile!"

Dorla told me this story recently. Had she smacked me or told me off?

"No," she said. "The girls forgave you because you were a little white kid with blond hair and they thought you were sweet."

From our first home I saw the mission school, almost unchanged since my childhood—dilapidated, but still in use. I was the only European child at the school, but I didn't feel strange, because the African kids didn't treat me as different from themselves. I almost felt African. In the playground we girls used to kneel in a circle and play a complex game with six smooth stones, moving them around rhythmically, according to strict rules, while we sang:

> *"Ah, ah, ah, ah!*
> *Malandiwe!*
> *Mary Makakosiwe!"*

The song had a monotonous, repetitive tune like a stuck record clicking, but it never bothered me, because we had to concentrate so deeply on the manual skills of the game.

Were they short of classrooms in my first year at school? I don't know, but I do remember having some lessons in the open air and learning to write by drawing letters in the earth. We would watch as our teacher drew the shape of a letter in the air before we wrote it with one finger in the dust. After he'd checked it for accuracy we would write it again, brushing out the first letter with the sides of our hands. Later we advanced to slates and slate pencils. When we needed to rub out something we spat on the slates and rubbed at the letters with our fingers until it was clean again.

Our classrooms were freezing cold on winter mornings. There were holes in the walls, ready for the fitting of windows, but there were no windows. Green blackboard paint was applied to the cement wall at the front of the classroom, but the wall was uneven and the chalk used to skid all over the place. Mrs. Mazlingana, our teacher, never stopped shouting. We had to be on our toes all the time. We shouted too, as we called out our rote-learned words and numbers. When I married Malcolm in 1969 Mrs. Maz. gave us two half-crowns, about fifty cents. It was a gift of riches from the heart of poverty.

The next building we passed was Dad's old office on the other side of the road from our "new" house. We had no phone in the house, but there was one in Dad's office, so if I wanted to phone my friends in the evenings I had to run across in the hugely silent dark, terrified of snakes or leopards or stray dogs.

We drove past other missionaries' houses down past the dairy. The powerful cow-pat smell brought back to me the childhood risks of being kicked during the milking, or whipped by a tail; and sloshing into my memory came the swisha-swish sounds of the milk as it hit the sides of the tin pail, the milk frothing as it almost overflowed the huge milk cans. Flies used to career around in the froth, but we all drank the milk (it was warm, straight from the cow) and were never ill to my knowledge, although I felt a bit uneasy about it once I'd heard of Louis Pasteur. The dairyman was aptly named Porridge.

At last, the church itself. I could feel the ghost of small-me inside it, everywhere. When I was little, the missionaries (all white) sat in special pews to the side of the pulpit. I was always puzzled by the fact that we didn't sit with the Africans. My egalitarian Australian parents were concerned about it too, but the mission had developed under the English tradition of a paternalistic set of behaviors toward "the natives," so they acted according to the rules for a while. Eventually my parents' Australianness created an alternative social climate, which meant that African friends felt so at ease with us that they didn't feel uncomfortable coming to meals or dropping by for a yarn. And we sat with the Africans in church.

In the church on the Sunday that we went back, the African men as usual sat to the left, the women to the right, and the young people in the middle pews. I don't know why. We, the only whites, sat in the middle, which meant a stereo effect of voices during the hymn singing: rich deep voices to the left and thrilling high voices to the right in harmonies so soulful that I felt I'd found heaven. I did cry. I always cry when I go back now because I don't live there anymore. Africa is my past, not my home.

Because I was fluent in Ndebele until I was six, when we went back to Australia for a year, I can still read hymns and pronounce the words correctly, but I don't know what I'm singing about! There's no organ in the church, nor a piano, so one woman's voice begins each hymn, setting the pitch and the rhythm. After the collection that Sunday morning, the old women returned to their seats dancing, swaying their arms above their heads, and smiling at me: Welcome back.

During the sermon, which I couldn't understand, I gazed

15

at the words written in a rainbow shape above the cross on the front wall. As a child I was never quite sure how many syllables there were in the third word. I used to concentrate really hard and try to count them, so for old time's sake I did it again: *Ukubongwa Makube Kunkulunkulu.* It means, "Let there be thanks to the Lord of Lords."

Outside the church afterwards I was greeted with amazement. "Is this Merri? Sure! The firstborn! Heh!" The familiar faces, the old friends, the dignity of these people made me think, "I'm home. I'm really home. This is where I belong." It isn't, not anymore, but it was comforting to pretend for a while. The handshaking continued, re-creating old relationships, making me long to stay. (When Zimbabwean Africans know each other well they shake hands in a special way, first as we do, then by grasping each others' thumbs, and then "normally" once again. Also, when they first meet someone, it's polite form for them to hold their right forearms in the cradle of their left hands as they move forward to shake hands. This custom is an old one leftover from the Matabele warrior days: it shows that they have no spear in either hand.)

On our way home from the church we passed the creek under the willows. As little kids at the mission school we'd have to toil down to the creek in the heat of the day to gather mounds of thick black clay, which we'd then mold into cattle and dry in the sun. I guess that was our art lesson. The heavy black clay, wet in my hands, always felt slimy as I squelched it through my fingers and my cattle never looked like cattle—more like giraffes or dogs.

The last, best thing at Hope Fountain just around the bend from the willows is the cattle dip. Ticks on cattle were such an ever-present problem that every Saturday morning all the herds of cattle from the farms on the mission used to thunder down the hill past our place to be dipped in a ghastly-smelling, tick-killing solution. We followed them. We'd identified a few cows in each herd and given them names and we shouted to each other when we recognized them every week.

"Look, look, there's Pooh Bum!"

"Yeah, and there's Doris Day!"

The herd boys whistled, and cracked their whips and yelled at the cattle as they prodded them with sticks down the slope into the disgusting chemical sloshing in a huge drain below. The terrified animals were forced to swim through the dip one by one, their heads straining upwards above the stinking water, panic rolling in their eyes. Sometimes they'd slip on the sloping exit and flounder backwards into the water again while we, half scared and half exhilarated, shouted encouragement.

I was barefoot, of course, and would occasionally step—splat!—into a pile of cow dung, which I'd scrape off with grass as best I could. I couldn't wash it off, since the creek, like most rivers and dams, had bilharzia snails in it, which would have given me bilharzia, a disease that causes sleepiness. We never paddled, washed, or swam in the creeks or dams, no matter how hot it was. My mother once made my middle sister, Jan, undergo extensive tests for bilharzia because she was always tired. Of course she was tired—she used to read under the bed covers late into the night.

The missionary families on Hope Fountain were my much-loved, and loving, extended family. By the time I was eight, there were four families with thirteen offspring

17

between them. Seven of us were similar in age and used to hang around together, riding bikes, going on picnics, exploring the bush, climbing rocks, playing in the cemetery, running around inside the church, playing school in the mission classrooms during the holidays, riding donkeys and horses, and messing about at the dairy and under the willows. We lived and played in each other's houses. The kindest of the mothers was "Auntie" Ruth Main. Hordes of us kids would descend upon her once or twice a day in the holidays, famished and thirsty. As we threw our bikes against the house she'd put the kettle on and make mounds of jam sandwiches that we devoured with the gratitude of locusts before we set off again.

There was always plenty to do. We were crazy about cars, so we all learned to drive as early as we could. We'd go to the drive-in to see films like *West Side Story,* and just before we arrived some of us would pile into the boot so we wouldn't have to pay. In the summer holidays I used to navigate on car rallies, loving the tension, counting the minutes in a tight voice, screaming as we screeched around corners or drove over rocky terrain. Brenda Lee was our favorite singer and "Blueberry Hill" our favorite song—we used to sing it hanging out of car windows. Love and sex also featured spasmodically in our lives and constantly in our conversation.

It all seems long ago now, although I remember it well. The memories are most clear on the grand occasions of my life such as the launch of *Sail Away* in Fremantle, the *Possum Magic* concert in the Adelaide Festival Centre or the N.S.W. Premier's Literary Awards in the Sydney Opera House, when I've stood in front of mirrors all dressed up in confused amazement, asking, "Are you really the same person as the one who used to yell around the cattle dip on a Saturday morning? Is it possible?"

It must be, since the past travels with us, no matter what masks we wear in the present.

The second essence of childhood in Africa was my schooling. After my first year at the mission school I was sent to a European school, since whites had to be educated in white schools, by law. I had to wear black lace-up shoes every day. My feet were astonished. The white kids didn't like me and I didn't like them. They poked fun at my strong Ndebele accent and copied the way I talked, but after that first year my feet resigned themselves to their imprisonment in unfamiliar surroundings and so did I. From that time on I had no close friends who were black until I was grown-up, because that was how the society worked.

My primary school, Hillside, was only eleven miles from the mission, in the suburbs of Bulawayo, the second-biggest city in what was then Southern Rhodesia. The image of sleazy, exotic colonial outposts in those old black-and-white films is out of place: Bulawayo is alive with tropical color and self-assured in its status as a city. When it was first settled by Europeans in the mid-nineteenth century, ox wagons were the chief form of transport. Turning them required skill and wide spaces, so the streets were made very broad in order to accommodate them. The spacious streets remain, giving central Bulawayo an expansive charm and graciousness. It has gorgeous parks, an excellent museum, several public libraries, a theater, cinemas, department stores, and markets. I didn't grow up in "wildest Africa," although I like to give the impression I did because it sounds so much more exciting.

In fact Bulawayo was rather like a smaller Adelaide with black faces.

My secondary school, Townsend Girls High School, was run along the lines of an English public school: prefects and "ordermarks," hymns every morning from *Ancient and Modern;* a strict uniform code; compulsory gym, swimming, and tennis in the summer, and Scottish dancing, netball, and hockey in the winter; eight O-level subjects until the end of Form Four, then three A-level subjects for two years. Our exams were marked in England and had to be posted airmail, so we wrote them on airmail-weight paper in the height of summer, the sweat from our hands making the paper warp and bubble.

I wasn't a memorable student, but I did manage to pass O level with six subjects, although I had to repeat Latin. I was keen to study drama at Bristol University at the time, for which O-level Latin was a prerequisite. In spite of my knowledge of Latin and my being consistently at the top of the class as a writer, I never showed any interest in or aptitude for grammar exercises out of context. I loathed sentence analysis, could rarely identify parts of speech, and dreaded comprehension and precis. Reading was different. I lost my heart to literature, having been enthusiastically introduced to vast amounts of it by my parents and my English teacher, Joh Smith.

Miss Smith was single, but it was impossible to think of her in spinsteresque terms. She must have been in her forties when she taught me, but her age was indefinable and irrelevant, since she communicated literary information in the form of gossip, which we all found irresistible. The short curls that squatted on top of her head were out of proportion to her lofty height and large nose. During the five years that she taught me, her love of literature often got the better of her. She'd collapse in tears as she read us poems like Browning's "Fra Lippo Lippi" or Byron's "Prisoner of Chillon."

"Girls," she'd sniff from behind her damp handkerchief, "one of you will have to read on. I can't, for the moment. God! It's so beautiful, isn't it?"

And it was. Her passion bulldozed any resistance we might have had for so-called "difficult" works. She *breathed* literature, making it a living force in our young lives, and hers, no matter when it had been written. She introduced Thomas Hardy in the year most of us turned fourteen.

"Imagine, girls. A man urinates against a wall and his whole life changes. A love story, a terrible coincidence, a series of mistakes and there you have it: a life in tatters. This book is called *The Mayor of Casterbridge*. Now who'd like to start reading?"

When I went to university as a mature-age student I was affronted to hear a negative assessment of Shelley's poetry. I remembered how Miss Smith, back in 1963, had stopped in midreading, during her introduction of the "Ode to the West Wind."

"Girls, listen. Close your eyes and listen. See! Words are the poets' paint. They're like musicians' notes:

' . . . *Thou*
For whose path the Atlantic's level powers

Cleave themselves into chasms, while far below
The sea-blooms and the oozy woods which wear
The sapless foliage of the ocean, know

21

Thy voice, and suddenly grow grey with fear,
And tremble and despoil themselves: O hear!' "

We heard. And since then I've often rolled the sound of those "oozy woods" around the walls of my literary bank, longing to appropriate them for my own use.

At Miss Smith's encouragement I threw myself into the dramatic society. She directed me in *Twelfth Night*, during which I discovered the life in Shakespeare before anyone had time to tell me that in some schools they could find only death. I played Malvolio and found out that with a little help from Shakespeare I could make an audience laugh until it cried. (Across the seas in a little Lincolnshire village my husband-to-be was also playing Malvolio. He too was discovering the life in Shakespeare and finding out how easy it was, with a little help from Shakespeare, to make an audience laugh until it cried.) After that, and partly because of my deep voice, Miss Smith cast me in men's comic roles such as Mr. Hardcastle in Goldsmith's *She Stoops to Conquer* and the bourgeois gentleman in Molière's *Bourgeois Gentilhomme*. I loved it.

My mother also cast me in her performances. She used to persuade me to tell stories in church like "The Story of the Other Wise Man" by Henry van Dyke and although I pretended a reluctance I was always secretly pleased to find myself in front of the congregation. She gave me plenty of opportunity to develop the power of communication. When I was ten I made up a rhyme that my sister still teases me about because she says I haven't changed:

When I act
Or when I sing
Or when I dance
I seem to be
In a peculiar trance.

By the time I was fourteen I had already experienced the thrill of being able to hush an audience and make it sit forward, or back, or suddenly jump, or sigh with satisfaction. Although my heart still beats at dangerous speeds before any kind of performance, including teaching my first class at the start of a new year, there's always a wild beat of longing-to-begin counterpointing the rhythm of nerves. Jan's right, I haven't changed.

By Lower Sixth I'd become stubbornly stagestruck and had decided to relax, academically, for the rest of my school career. The pressure for good results lessened as soon as I'd made up my mind not to go to university, but to make a grand entrance at drama school instead. My parents were appalled by my mulishness. They must have known that I had a brain (although I genuinely doubted it myself at the time) and must have been fearful that I'd waste it. I lacked academic confidence, and the idea of three years' more study at that point in my life wearied me. The only serious arguments I ever had with my parents reverberated round the house at that time. My grandfather in Adelaide removed the financial barrier to my ambition by offering to pay my fees and living expenses, so all I had to do was to pass A level and find a drama school to take me in. At school I did just enough work to get by, sang in the choir, threw my weight

around as a prefect and a house captain, chaired the Sixth
Form Forum (a current-affairs arena set up by our history
teacher), and entered public-speaking competitions run by
the Royal Commonwealth Society, and won. My mother
helped me write the speeches. The finale of this drama was
that I passed my three A levels, English, French, and history,
as successfully as many of my classmates did: that is, only just.

The tone of my schooling wasn't far removed from the
Angela Brazil school stories to which I'd once been addicted,
but I have few complaints other than the lack of opportunity
to interact sensibly with the Opposite Sex, owing to its
unfortunate absence from our classes. We tended to think
of boys as beautiful beings, young gods even, for whom we'd
do almost anything. When we met them at interschool func-
tions we were stupefied with misplaced admiration. The men
now who were boys then must still have an enormous feeling
of self-importance because we gave it to them so whole-
heartedly.

In 1963 my best friend, Barbara Bacon, and I formed a
singing duo called the Barberrions (a spelling based on a
combination of our names). Barbara's voice was rich and
strong, and her ability to harmonize extraordinary. My voice
wasn't as strong, but I could sing in tune fairly pleasantly.
We sang folk songs on television and had a few gigs around
the place. One night we sang at an army camp out of town
to two hundred soldiers on National Service. They hadn't
seen a female, let alone two, for six weeks. The wolf whistles
made us feel like film stars. This was, of course, prior to our
feminist awakening. In Rhodesia in the early sixties the feminists were as deeply asleep as the Sleeping Beauty. Apart
from my mother, that is. She was *wide* awake.

In the same year, 1963, our school music teacher formed a nine-voice choir, the Barbara Thomas Singers. Barbara Bacon and I sang alto. The songs were traditional and classical: exquisite three-part pieces that were a challenging contrast to the musical repertoire of the Barberrions. We performed on special occasions and at special places such as the governor's residence or the town hall, feeling mighty talented and oh, so grand.

Growing up in Africa didn't mean growing up intellectually stunted. My schooling was more than adequate, and more than tolerable, and what it didn't teach me, my parents did.

I found the third essence of my childhood in our house, in which I ruled the roost until I was four years old, when my sister Jan was born. I didn't feel put out at the time. It wasn't until her exceptional intelligence made itself apparent that I felt put out. She was five and I was nine when she explained loftily to me, her elder and better, a piece of information about the Greek gods. I was impressed and reported the conversation to my parents. Almost immediately afterwards I felt an uncharacteristic dagger of self-doubt. Then jealousy. Then inferiority. I wasn't Jan's elder and better after all. I was her elder and lesser, and I've never recovered from that demeaning realization although I now suffer it more cheerfully.

We were good companions only after our lights had been put out, when we'd talk and giggle for hours, ignoring as unimportant noise Mum's frequent yells to go to sleep. In the daytimes of our lives we saw as little of each other as possible. In order to get into her room Jan had to pass through mine, so I drew a chalk line along the floor and told her never to cross it, or else. She was quiet, studious, and self-contained. At thirteen she enraged me by reading *War and Peace* on the long plane journey from Africa to Australia. We all knew she was clever, but I couldn't see why she had to be so ostentatious about it.

When I was ten and Jan was six our sister Alison Gail was born. We were meant to call her Gail; she, however, christened herself Lailu. (In her twenties she reverted to Alison.) Because I was ten when she came into our lives she was like a doll to me and I adored her and fussed over her and showed her off to my friends with great pride. I can't remember her impinging much on my life after I started high school, and by the time I left home at eighteen, when she was eight, I was only dimly aware of her existence as a dear little kid who looked up to me. I wrote her patronizing letters from drama school because our age difference was too great for me to regard her as anything other than my sweet baby sis. It was only as an adult that the word *sisterhood* expanded its meaning beyond the Women's Liberation Movement to include the love, friendship, and company of my parents' other daughters.

(I will hardly mention my sisters again. Jan lives in London, Lailu in Adelaide. Both of them have married twice, very happily the second time, and Lailu has a daughter, Tamara. When Lailu was twenty-three she became a paraplegic; but the story of my sisters' woes and joys is theirs to tell, not mine to steal.)

Although there were only five in our family we always had two African people working for us: a house girl and a garden boy. The house girl was usually a woman and the garden boy a man, so Mum wouldn't use the words *servant*, *nanny, house girl,* or *garden boy*—she felt they were demeaning. She always called them "our helpers," but I'm still embarrassed by that euphemism. It can't hide the fact that these people did a great deal of work for a small deal of pay. I never did any housework except make my bed and occasionally dry the dishes, and I used to be irritated when my ornaments were dusted and put back in the wrong places on the shelf. I had no realization of how lucky I was not to have to dust the shelf myself.

On the dining-room table we kept a small brass bell shaped like a curled claw. When the first course needed to be cleared away one of us rang the bell and the house girl came in from the kitchen, took away the dirty dishes, and then brought in the next course. I took this pretty much for granted until I came home from drama school for the Christmas holidays in 1966. When my mother rang the bell I went red to the roots of my hair, newly aware of our privileged way of life. I now have the bell as a symbol of my colonial past.

I remember one house girl in particular whom I adored. Her name was Zodwa. We'd have long chats when I dried the dishes in the evening and then I'd sit with her and help her eat her *sadza,* a very thick porridge made from cornmeal, the diet staple of Zimbabwean Africans. She taught me African songs. She also tried to teach me African dance movements. We'd use the broom as a pretend spear, but her dances were not in my white bones and she'd laugh unkindly at my attempts. I must have picked up something, however, because my family tells me I still dance like an upbeat Matabele warrior.

At seventeen I had a boyfriend at boarding school to

27

whom I wrote long letters every day. They were drivel of course and practice made the banality perfect. He always replied. My fluency as a writer developed as rapidly as the relationship and even surpassed it. We were often tongue-tied face-to-face. The mail in our house was left on top of the fridge, so every lunchtime, hot and sweaty from school, I'd make for the fridge straight away. Sometimes there'd be no letter and I'd be crestfallen until I noticed Zodwa trying to keep a straight face.

"Zodwa, did Andrew write to me today?"

"Not today, Merri. He doesn't love you anymore."

"ZODWA!!!"

Suddenly a letter would appear from behind her back and we'd leap around the kitchen as she held it high above her head, out of my reach, laughing.

I often wonder what it was really like for Zodwa, working in our house. The breakfast table was always set by 6:00 A.M. and breakfast was served by 6:10. She did all the cleaning, washing, ironing, and tidying, and the occasional bit of child minding as well. (My mother always did the cooking.) In the afternoon from about 2:00 to 4:00 she rested, but I'm sure there were some nights when she was still working at 8:00. It must have been a very tiring day.

Although we grew up in Africa, under a British education system, we were never allowed to forget that we were Australian. My mother had given us to understand that Australia was the most wonderful place on earth and when we returned for long visits in '52, '59, and '63, this chauvinism was confirmed. I enjoyed attending the Demonstration School in Armidale, N.S.W. in Year Two, and in Year Nine spent contrasting terms at the easygoing Mount Barker High in the Adelaide Hills, and the frightfully correct Hornsby Girls High in Sydney. My parents' friends were educated, fascinating people, and the east coast swarmed with likable cousins. Australia wasn't home, but for us it was close to Heaven because of the sea: Zimbabwe is a landlocked country. Everyone we met was generous and friendly. Our experiences were all positive.

When I came back to Australia in 1970, I was taken aback to discover how many people weren't ecstatic to be Australian and learned with amazement that there was a phenomenon known as "the cultural cringe." It made me angry and still does.

During my childhood, Australian friends sent us Australian reading material: the classics of Australian childhood such as *Shy the Platypus* by Leslie Rees, *The Australian Book* by Eve Pownall, the Billabong books by Mary Grant Bruce, *Snugglepot and Cuddlepie* by May Gibbs, and everyone's favorite koala book: *Blinky Bill* by Dorothy Wall. I was steeped in all things Australian. We were sent Minties at Christmas; Mum made us lamingtons and Anzac biscuits and raved about the Holden being "Australia's own car"; we sang "The Road to Gundagai" on long car journeys. We listened to aboriginal Dreamtime stories on 45 r.p.m. records and laughed at (till we knew by heart) a Barry Humphries record called "Wild Life in Suburbia." I still have it.

From the Billabong books I advanced to adult books because there wasn't much in between. Some of the times I remember best in our house were reading long novels uninterrupted during our afternoon rests when we'd lie on our beds for about an hour to escape the afternoon heat. I read adult books because they were there, row upon row on the bookshelves. My favorites were Jane Austen's *Pride and Prejudice*; Dickens's *Dombey and Son* and *Tale of Two Cities*, and Flaubert's *Madame Bovary*. (The delights of so-called *popular* fiction were only introduced to me in my thirties.) In the wet season, between November and March, I'd deliberately lose myself in a book as afternoon storms lashed the lowering sky and hammered the ground. The noise on the corrugated iron roof deafened me with fright, so I'd snuggle deeply into the time and place of my book for safety.

My first book (never published of course) was written during a storm, when I was ten. Outside, much to my consternation, since I'd been made environmentally conscious at school, precious topsoil was being swept down the hillside in rivers. I wrote a book to explain why this was a bad thing and read it to Mum as she plucked a chicken for dinner the next day. She said absentmindedly, "That's lovely, darling," thereby providing me with every writer's deepest wish: an appreciative, uncritical audience. "I can write!" I thought and was pleased. Even thrilled. But it didn't make me prolific. My next effort, a "novel" about race relations that filled an exercise book and made me cry, was written when I was fourteen. My third book, the first published, came out when I was thirty-seven. That was *Possum Magic*.

My enjoyment of poetry, which began at home but was also nurtured at school, stemmed from a series of records of poetry spoken by John Gielgud, some of which I learned off by heart, enticed by the musical sound of Gielgud's intonations. To this day I can recite "Break, Break, Break" by Alfred Lord Tennyson and the "Journey of the Magi" by T.S. Eliot, exactly as Gielgud recited them. I think poetry appealed to me because I was attracted to its sound first.

One winter's morning when I was home from school with a bad cold I took off the shelf a book of poems by Rupert Brooke and read it hunched up in my eiderdown beside an open fire. Inside was a pencil drawing of the young Rupert looking exactly as I'd imagined a poet should look: vulnerably artistic. I adored him and learned some of his poems, the open book clutched to my chest, memorizing appealing lines. One I've never forgotten is "She quacked in flat platitudes beside me . . ." because it was my first discovery, suddenly, that words could mimic sounds, and I was thrilled by the possibilities it opened up.

All my childhood I was exposed to the music of the Bible. The sound of the often-repeated words in all the church services I attended affected me forever, as a speaker and a writer. The sonorousness, the position of words, the number of words per phrase, the rhythms of those phrases, and the placement of the pauses have been collected in a storehouse from which I draw constantly, particularly for opening and closing sentences. Listening to the Bible developed my need to read aloud every sentence I write in order to check its balance and meaning. When I read or write, I *hear*. The words I've read ring in my ears and reverberate against the ceilings of my storehouse, echoing their way into my own writing. Earlier in this chapter, for example, in a description of my mission classroom I wrote: "There were holes in the walls, ready for the fitting of windows, but there were no windows." Even as I wrote "but there were no windows" I knew I'd heard that phrasing before. Days later I remembered its source: T.S. Eliot's "The Rock," in which this line occurs: "But there was no water, only rock." I even stole the *w* of his water for my windows! But that's all right—it was Eliot himself who said good writers steal, bad writers borrow.

I know why I became such an avid reader, but I'm trying to pinpoint the way we used language in our family—because I can't stop talking. I must have had early practice somewhere and evening mealtimes stand out in my memory. The five of us would talk and talk and talk until long after the table had been cleared. Politics was a constant topic of conversation. Our family's political beliefs and our values differed from those of most other whites in Zimbabwe. Occasionally I'd have violent arguments at school trying to persuade my friends that Africans were like us, except they were black, and I even got into a scratching, hitting fight once across a couple of desks. Africans had been rioting for better conditions and had been controlled by policemen handling whips and Alsatians. The brother of one of my friends was a policeman who thought he'd done a hero's job that day so of course his sister was proud of him and said so. It was too much for me; I snapped. Usually I kept quiet about our political leanings because I knew I'd lose friends if I spoke out. It's easy for a fifteen-year-old to be a Judas, but I often felt guilty about my cowardice. I'm bolder now because it's more acceptable to be antiapartheid.

My mother on the other hand was foolhardy. She'd write letters to the paper about the iniquity of censorship, but they'd never get published. Instead there'd be a blank space on the letters page with a statement in the middle of it saying, "This letter was about censorship. It has been censored." I don't know what enormity she finally committed, but eventually the Smith regime banned her from teaching on the grounds that she was subversive. I felt nervous. If they'd been watching her, had they been watching all of us? But I also felt proud. Good old Mum! Fancy being banned!

When our house wasn't a hotbed of political ferment it was a haven of culture and peace. My memories of homework are always attached to classical music. In the evening Dad would play recordings of Mozart, Bach, Beethoven, Haydn, Brahms, and others while he read and Mum wrote. What did she write? Letters? Stories? She never told us. But from a young age I noticed her doing it, took in the fact that people wrote for pleasure, and tried it myself from time to time, with satisfying results.

There were pictures on all the walls in our house, framed prints of paintings by well-known artists, but the best room of all was the loo. Dad had a thing about Van Gogh. One year he framed the twelve prints from a Van Gogh calendar and hung them in there. People who used our gallery always talked about it afterwards.

My father trained teachers. Like father like daughter. His students doted on him. He's now attending weddings of their *grand*children. Both he and his students tell me he was an excellent teacher with high expectations and a wonderful sense of humor. When I began anxiously and unexpectedly to teach, he comforted me with his maxim: "Don't teach. Let the students learn." His most famous colleague on Hope Fountain in the late 1940s was the current Prime Minister of Zimbabwe, Robert Mugabe. I'm sure I value teaching more than I do writing as a career because in our house teaching was such a highly respected profession.

When we were young, my father's stomach ulcers and migraines revealed the strain of his attempt to do the best job with the least resources in a difficult political climate.

Frustration caused by lack of proper facilities led him to write educational textbooks with Third World conditions in mind. My own favorite is *What Is Good Teaching?* In the new feminist age he'd probably prefer to retitle the one called *A Headmaster and His School.* In the mid-sixties he left the missionary society, went on a world fund-raising tour of major religious and aid organizations, and set up the combined-churches, world-class United Teachers' College, for Africans. At sixty-six he retired and retrained as a librarian. (My book *Wilfrid Gordon McDonald Partridge* has provided this latter-day librarian with the bliss of a *personal* I.S.B.N. number!) In 1988, when he was seventy-six, the Library Association of Great Britain published his latest book, *Low Cost Librarianship,* also written with the Third World in mind.

In character I'm like my father, detesting arguments, thinking well of myself, working without ceasing, seeing the brighter side of any situation, and spending money as though the Biblical verse "Unto him who hath, it shall be given" were God's explicit permission to be absolutely reckless. But in personality I am my mother myself. She's incredibly friendly and will chat warmly to total strangers in any queue, a habit regarded with deep suspicion in England, where most people in queues pray to fade unnoticed into the grayness. Happily, her strong Sydney accent reveals her to be merely foreign, not mad. Like me, she's full of laughter, noisy, and excitable, the antithesis of calm. She's also the tough type who says that the only worrying thing about bodysurfing is the possibility of losing one's false teeth in the waves. Unlike me, she abhors sentimentality. "Ah, slop!" she groans when people kiss in films. And unlike me, she's a chronic insomniac. One night when there seemed to be burglars thumping about in the house, I got up to investigate, but it was only Ma, doing yoga on the sitting-room floor at three A.M.

However, there's another side to her: Nan, the Writer and Intellectual. In 1970 a trust fund was set up in South Africa in memory of Archbishop of Cape Town Joost de Blank, a courageous worker against apartheid. My mother was the first recipient of the Joost de Blank Award in 1971, which enabled her to write and publish a novel called *Not Alone*, based on an anthropological study of urban African family life. Her second novel, *To Breathe and Wait*, came out in 1986, when she was age seventy-three, and as I write this in 1991 she's across the world putting the finishing touches to *Easy to Say*, a book of meditations on the Lord's Prayer. So when it comes to careers, I haven't been a Great Explorer of New Realms. The theater was just a token tiptoe through the tollgate into the unknown and back again. As soon as I returned to the safety of my own home, I tried on the colorful careers of my parents and found they fitted very comfortably on my unadventurous shoulders.

We went to church and Sunday school every week, we said grace before meals (*Benedictus benedicat, per Jesum Christum Dominum Nostrum*), and we read from a children's book of prayers each night in bed, each sister taking turns to read the responses, but I never felt constrained by church, religion, or being a missionary's child. I don't go to church much anymore, but Methodist values still wind me up and send me ticking into my daily life. That's why I drink alcohol rarely and without pleasure, work much more constantly and conscientiously than is necessary, fill in tax forms with an honesty bordering on folly, forgive people when smashing them in the face is really my heart's desire, cope stoically with illness when enjoying it should be perfectly acceptable, feel guilty about enjoying the luxuries of first-class hotels (why aren't I giving the money to the poor?), stagger around under the burdensome knowledge that serving others ought to be my raison d'être, and feel a nagging worry if I'm having a good time, because if I am, there must be something wrong somewhere.

Academic success was considered important in our household, but I gave up on that at nine because of Jan's emerging brilliance. My school days were pleasant and packed, but as I've explained, I did the minimum of work. This was partly so that Jan and I could never be compared on an equal basis. She was so bright that Lailu languished in her shadow and didn't begin to realize her potential until she was nearly thirty. I wanted people to believe that if I put my mind to it I could be as academically bright as Jan was, but in my heart of hearts I had grave doubts as to my ability. When I ask myself why I'm now so driven to succeed, I come to the conclusion that it's partly an irrational and continuing competition between myself and Jan for parental approval.

Jan and I began on different careers, she as an educational psychologist and I as an actress, but we've both ended up lecturing in teachers' colleges, with the same academic textbooks on our shelves, and attending the same conferences. At an international conference on the teaching of writing in Norwich in 1985, we decided to have a bit of fun one day by appearing identically dressed in red T-shirts, red-and-white-striped overalls, red socks, and red shoes. Our hair was, for once, similar in style and color. We looked like twins. The impact we made at breakfast was so much greater than we'd expected that we almost lost our nerve. We de-

cided to brazen it out, however, but sat far apart in our first
session. The speaker, from New York, was introduced. Minutes later in disbelief she noticed us and stopped in mid-
sentence to remark dryly, "I take it you two know each
other."

"Sisters." We grinned.

Because our parents are who they are, Jan and Lailu and
I have an overactive work ethic ruling our days. We're organized achievers. We're productive, not passive, members
of our respective communities, having been brought up to
believe in the sanctity of hard work and the disgrace of not
using our talents. I look askance at wealthy men's wives who
don't have jobs outside the home. It's not their fault they're
so fortunate, but with a mother like mine I can't help being
shaken by their daring.

Another strong influence from my parents is my distrust
of wealth: "It is easier for a camel to go through the eye of
a needle than for a rich man to enter the kingdom of God."
I'm nervous about earning as much as I do for writing while
at the same time holding down a well-paid position in a
university. I don't really feel that my soul's in danger, but
there's always a gnawing at the back of my mind about being
well-off, as if it were somehow immoral and my own sinful
fault. Perhaps that's one reason why Malcolm and I spend
invisibly, as it were, on air travel: because it isn't concretely
ostentatious—no one else can actually see where the money's
gone. I guess I'm troubled by being "comfortable." It's almost
as if I've contracted a disease.

Throughout my childhood, because we were not well-off
and therefore had to live very simply, I thought we belonged
to an underprivileged class of society. I thought we were

working-class, but I had no understanding of the word *class*.
It was only when I went to England and saw my childhood
from afar that I realized how privileged I'd been and how
fortunate I was to have grown up in a home in which emotional safety was matched with cultural richness and intellectual stimulation.

But I didn't go to England immediately.

3

Made in Switzerland

School came to an end and tossed me into the world in December 1964. Drama school, the chocolate of my education, began in October '65. Separating these events was a six-month stay in Switzerland from which I never recovered.

Although I'd been given permission to audition for drama school my parents brooded about it. My father revealed his reservations one day in a chance heart-to-heart with the vice-chancellor of the University of Rhodesia.

"Daughters!" he must have said, with a sad little shrug.

"Drama school! Even if she completes the course she'll end up without any academic qualifications."

As luck would have it the vice-chancellor had also suffered a stagestruck daughter. "Send her to Rose Bruford's, in London," he said. "That's what we did. There's a compulsory teaching course alongside the acting. First-class institution and a recognized teaching diploma at the end of it."

The chocolate was within reach. I had to grab it! I auditioned for the Rose Bruford College of Speech and Drama by audiotape from my don't-come-near-me bedroom. Seven hundred others also applied for the fifty available places that year, but two places were always reserved for overseas students and one of those opportunities was given to me. Perhaps only two of us applied. I was informed that I'd be regarded as a risk, unseen as I was, and almost unheard, from Africa. My situation would be reviewed at the end of the first term and if I were deemed to be without talent I'd be asked to leave immediately. I decided to risk it.

So drama school was organized, but there remained the question of what to do in the blank months before it began. An overseas visitor told us about the Blue Angels at the Château de Bossey in Switzerland, a conference center for the World Council of Churches, outside Geneva. Blue Angels were volunteers who came from all over the world to work as maids in the center for six months at a time. They were "angels" because they slaved for nothing, except pocket money, board, and lodging, and "blue" because of the color of their uniform. I applied and was accepted. Five days before my nineteenth birthday I said good-bye to my youth and flew away to Europe.

Why did no one foresee the danger in this Rite of Passage? Why did no one suggest that Switzerland of all places was the last country to which I should have been sent? Why did no warning bells clang when my plane touched down in the wintry air? To explain the full horror of the Swiss impact on my character I need to backtrack a little.

Seven years prior to my momentous arrival in Switzerland, when I was only twelve, I'd achieved the Virginia Woolf nirvana of A Room of One's Own and with it had appeared, almost overnight, a weakness for tidiness that soon developed into a passion, inherited from my father. (My mother and sisters never allowed tidiness to interfere with their daily lives.) In my sanctuary everything had its place: slippers just so under the bed, ruler just so on the desk, brush and comb just so on the dressing table, and all the drawers organized to within a centimeter of their available space. It was then that I developed my continuing custom of laying out on a chair in symmetric rows and piles the clothes I have chosen to wear on the following day. My shoes, of course, were under the chair, always centered precisely. From that time onward I strove daily for order, neatness, and control. Tidiness became an affliction.

Thus afflicted, I entered the Château de Bossey in March 1965, unaware that it would prove to be my temperamental Paradise. My obsessions were ripe for reinforcement and it came from all directions, in particular from the German and Dutch housekeepers. For me it was pure heaven to have to fold the white tea towels as instructed so that the red stripes down the middle sat exactly aligned, one on top of the other, making a long, neat red stripe all the way down the cupboard.

Cleanliness was introduced to me with all the metaphorical whips one would expect of a Swiss institution. Filth had never had a high profile in my life, as I had grown up with servants who had cleaned on my behalf, but I arrived at the château in time for its annual spring cleaning and was taught to see dirt as carefully as an artist might see the details in an autumn leaf. Light fittings came down. Drawers were pulled out. Cupboards were stripped. Floors, walls, and ceilings were scrubbed. Curtains and rugs were beaten as if dust were a disease and a broom handle the cure. Cleanliness soon became another affliction, another drug, and I became a hopeless addict.

There were six Angels at Bossey at any one period. In my time there was a girl from England, another from Holland, one from Belgium, two from Germany, and me from miles away. Although four of this group could speak German, we spoke mostly French and a little English. We were roughly the same age and just out of school, so we spent our spare time together in each other's rooms, talking and laughing until late, drinking mint tea and gorging ourselves on Lindt chocolate. The building we lived in was separated from the main château by a cobblestoned yard. Whenever I wore clogs I was reminded of the Highwayman who clattered and clanged over the cobbles in the dark inn yard while Tim the ostler listened.

The château accommodated a new conference every week on a variety of religious or social issues. The world came to Bossey and we waited on it at table and made its beds: Greek Orthodox priests—the Greek writing on their toothpaste was a special fascination—German professors, French intellectuals, Italian social workers, Indian missionaries, African activists whom I gravitated towards, English bishops, and a host of other fascinating people. We were welcome at all the conference sessions but were usually too tired to attend.

Our day started at 7:00 A.M. and finished twelve hours later, with one morning off a week and a free day every fortnight. In spite of my soft upbringing I coped. Perhaps the work was a novelty at first. Setting fourteen tables, each with twelve places, three times a day, often became a game: we'd compete against each other, twelve forks in our left hands, twelve knives in our right, dropping them into their places as we raced around the tables to see who'd finish first. Tedious tasks flew by in friendship. As we hung never-ending basket loads of heavy wet sheets in cellars or attics or outside when summer arrived, we'd gossip away the boredom in a rattle of French that would have amazed our schoolteachers. Often we would sing. When we felt particularly oppressed we'd croon songs about chariots "comin' for to carry me home" and ask ourselves where all the flowers had gone.

Our cultures crossed and crisscrossed as we worked to-gether, cleaning rooms, scrubbing toilet bowls, laying out cups and saucers for afternoon tea—all the cup handles facing right, much to my ordered delight, and all the teaspoons in the same straight position behind each cup—waiting at ta-bles, washing up, drying up, cooking, picking cherries, beat-ing rugs, sweeping floors. We were strictly supervised and never allowed to slacken our pace. If a job happened to be finished earlier than expected another would be found to fill in the space, in case the devil found work for idle hands to do, I presumed with resentment. We were always tired. On our days off we slept until midday. When the six months ended we longed to sleep like Rip Van Winkle, undisturbed for a hundred years.

I had arrived in Switzerland as a tidy, well-organized, and relatively well-balanced school-leaver. I left it as a crazed young woman who would forever seek after cleanliness, tidiness, and order in the way that nuns seek after righteousness and truth. My manic quest for tidiness and pristine cleanliness means relaxation has become difficult, work is constant, and stress is always just around the corner. Although a cleaning woman helps with the heavy work once a week, the Movement Against Mess is a seven-day event that has to be conducted in her absence. The obsessions I developed still rampage daily through the house. I think I have out-Swissed the Swiss. Before I leave for work I make sure that the towels in the bathroom all hang at the same length. I leave the kitchen sink gleaming after breakfast, ready to smile and wink a welcome at the end of the day. Taps twinkle, teaspoons sparkle. I clean the outsides of toilet bowls, the insides of cupboard doors, the bottoms of mugs. I scrub the grooves on the toothpaste lid. I attack grubbiness on light switches. The unseen, greasy dust on top of my kitchen cupboards thinks mistakenly that it will be left alone. Old toothbrushes lie in wait to be used as weapons against the filth trying to accumulate behind the taps and around the plug holes. "Out, damn'd spot!" takes on a whole new meaning.

Our weekends run like noisy clockwork: towels and bath mats washed on Saturday, bed linen changed on Sunday. My family's resistance to this regimental discipline is feeble when faced with the force of my captaincy. The only defeat that I've accepted is the region beyond my daughter's closed bedroom door. To cross the battlefield into that no-mum's-land is more than I can manage this side of a straitjacket.

The legacy of Switzerland has helped me to manage a house, a family, and two careers without going off my head completely. It gives me sufficient efficiency to fight off the panic of busy days. Only in the worst moments of tiredness do I slip terrified into a despair of mismanagement. It makes me unafraid of hard work. It taught me how to invent time-saving routines. And it bequeathed me the most uncluttered desk I've ever encountered.

It was at this desk that I made my disturbing discovery about tidiness in relation to writing. As a writer I always wanted neatness and I wanted it fast. I wanted perfection and I wanted it now. I wanted *immediately* a shine in my writing equivalent to the shine on my bathroom taps. I wanted *immediately* a structure in my writing equivalent to the neat rows and piles of pillow slips and sheets in my linen cupboard. Wanting didn't make it happen. It was only when I was taught that the secret of good writing is rewriting that I dared to develop the untidiness that my drafts desperately needed.

Slowly I learned to lock away my hausfrau hang-ups before I sat down, pencil in hand, to start writing. Slowly I learned to remove Switzerland from the map of my memory before I attacked a clean piece of paper. Slowly I learned how to be messy when mess was required. I began crossing out, writing above the crossed-out words, writing sideways in the margins, allowing arrows to deface whole pages, drawing boxes around misplaced paragraphs, and writing notes to myself beside imperfectly expressed ideas. But I found it difficult. I had to steel myself to accomplish it. Because the tidiness of a word processor threatens my creativity I hand-write all my early drafts in pencil. It's only towards the end of a piece that I can transfer it to the screen of the Modern Age for a final bit of fiddling.

I'm sure the tendrils of influence from my Blue Angel Period will clutch at me forever. I was hopelessly conditioned long before it ended. When my six months came to a close, I was primed for life with all the precision and reliability of a Swiss watch. Off I went, out of the château and out of Switzerland—tick-tocking towards England and a new life, filled with drama.

4

Scenes from Drama School

I made my entrance at drama school playing the part of a plump nineteen-year-old who spoke with a Rhodesian accent and wore Hush Puppies, a pleated skirt, twin set, and pearls. I must have been acting. It couldn't have been me looking like that: no makeup, no attention-seeking hair, no confidence, no friends. In the student common room I scuttled into corners like a mouse hoping the sophisticats would leave me alone.

On the first day it was "Beginners onstage, please!" We were forced into a performance that would, for years to come, cause us to wake in fright and clutch our sleeping partners, screaming, "Take me away! Please take me away!" Second-and third-year students, mocking, hungry for the humiliation of those less fortunate than themselves, packed the stalls. Perched along a gallery at the back were the members of staff, their pens raised like poisonous arrows, ready to record our accents, speech defects, and vocal infelicities. Individually we had to read a poem and give a short speech about ourselves and our recent past. "Blue Angel" caused a hideous laugh. Group improvisations followed. The tension of the occasion caused one hapless student to forget himself so completely that he said, "It's pissing down outside." He was mortified and hardly spoke for the rest of the year. Howls of laughter issued from the stalls, not because he'd said *pissing*, but because he'd been mortified about it. *Pissing*, we were soon to learn, was not a shocking word at all. There were no shocking words. Within a week we were able to reflect on that first day and say, "Wasn't it fahking awful, darlings?"

Misery engulfed me often in the first few months. I was far from home without the sort of support that the Blue Angels had been able to give to each other. England was new and stiff and stuffy. Adults called me "Merrion," my long-forgotten real name, and I hated it. (My antipathy towards the name Merrion is largely due to the fact that it's so easy to get wrong. Besides, having been "Mem" for as long as I can remember, I no longer feel comfortable with the Merrion persona.) Drama school was new and demanding and outrageous. Fellow students called me "Darling!"—an anonymous name which contributed to my initial disorientation.

We lived in approved digs (lodgings) until we were Third

Years, when we graduated to flats of our own finding. My landlady was young and Cockney and always called me Marion because the Merrion was beyond her. When I needed company her raucous laughter and coarse jokes cheered me up. When I needed to practice storytelling or reading aloud her little girls provided an uncritical wide-eyed audience. When I went out she'd always say, "Mind 'ow ya go!" And when I came home late she'd wink and say, " 'Ave a good night, didja, Marion? I 'eard them milk bottles rattling on the doorstep at three o'clock this morning."

I came to Rose Bruford's staggering under the burden of my Protestant work ethic and my mania for tidiness and cleanliness. As if these disabilities weren't sufficient to cripple my personality, another was added: punctuality. Classes began at ten in the morning and finished at five. There were no free periods. A register was taken at the start of each session and anyone who was late was expelled. Expelled! So I am never late. Now, when the police catch me speeding and demand an explanation I feel like saying, "Well, it's like this, officer. At drama school . . ."

Rose Bruford was real. She'd founded her own drama school just after the Second World War and continued to teach in it until she retired in 1968, at the end of my third year. (We made our exits together.) Her entry into our lives was superbly theatrical. There we were, waiting for our first Mime and Movement class, sitting on the bare wooden floor of a large studio, nervously togged up in our brand-new black leotards, tights, and ballet shoes, and feeling like fools (especially the tough lads from Glasgow and Yorkshire), when in swept a diminutive woman similarly dressed, but all in

49

green, with a full-length green cloak that she cast aside with a single charismatic fling. Mentally we clapped. She was brilliant.

From Rose Bruford herself I learned mime, acting, and verse speaking. Mime and Movement was my least successful class (the Matabele warrior did battle with Marcel Marceau, and won), but her strict discipline and brusque encouragement developed in me a potential I didn't know I had. When she gave us demonstrations in verse-speaking classes, her rich voice and natural interpretation dazzled us. Poetry seemed as natural as prose when she spoke it. There was never a hint of the cloying preciousness that is so often the ruination of spoken verse. I longed for more, but unlike Oliver never dared to ask.

She ruled our lives with uncompromising sternness, missing nothing. In early 1966 Malcolm (Fox) and I were summoned to her office to explain why we had gone to Paris for a weekend together. How had she known? Wasn't our free time our own? When my hair was a bright dyed blond she slid towards me in a crowded room and whispered from the side of her mouth, "Merrion, do something about your hair." The following day I appeared with my hair as close to natural as I could remember. I was summoned to her office. I entered. She smiled. "Sit down." I sat. "Your hair looks lovely," she said. "You may go." I rose. "Thank you, Miss Bruford," I said. And almost curtsied.

We dreaded being "called up" by this dragon in her marvelous green spectacles, and whenever it happened the entire student body was agog to know who, and why, and what the result was. Pregnancy, for example, was punished by expulsion. Whether being pregnant was worse or better than being late in her hierarchy of sins we never knew. The sentence for the crime was the same.

Because we'd been accepted into drama school we arrived believing we could act, but our confidence was sapped for three hours every Wednesday afternoon in Acting Exercises. Each week we prepared for these classes by studying a chapter from *The Art of the Actor* by Stanislavsky. In class, Rose would use the exercises from the book, slapping our sleeping talent awake, making us come to terms with how little we knew, exposing our weaknesses in individual and group humiliation, and leading us towards new depths of truth in our acting, combining it with disciplined technique. (In America it is known as Method Acting.) We lived our acting roles as closely as possible by employing a phenomenon known as "emotion memory" in which we remembered as clearly as we could from our own lives the events most similar to those in the scene we were about to play. In this way our acting became closer to real, deeper, dragged from the very well of our being—way beyond the amateur stuff we'd all loved, when we'd overused our faces and voices.

There were fifty of us, twenty-five men and twenty-five women, in that first year, and we took Acting Exercises together. If, as I was, you were called on to mime looking for a needle stuck in a curtain, there was no escape. A hundred eyes, eager to find fault, watched, unblinking, in the appalling silence. It was much more alarming than being in a play. I've never been frightened of performance since, and never will be, unless someone asks me to search in silence for a nonexistent needle stuck nowhere in a nonexistent curtain.

In the end, Acting Exercises became my favorite class.

51

Everything (except Mime and Movement, Teaching Method, Greek Dance, the History of Education, Ballet, and Stage Management) became my favorite class. For half my lifetime I had longed to be at drama school, so I threw myself into it. Storytelling was heaven. Acting in plays was Paradise. Verse Speaking, Voice and Speech, Radio Technique—all these were Bliss.

In each of the three years of our training we suffered three thirteen-week terms. In addition to our all-day-no-free-period timetable, we often rehearsed two evenings a week. In our third year we were also committed to Saturday-morning Children's Theater. Spare time at home was spent on voice and speech exercises ("M-m-m-m-m-m-m-aaaah"), learning lines, rehearsing stories, and practicing poems. Spare time at College, before 10:00 A.M. and after 5:00 P.M., was used for the rehearsing group work that we'd have to present in class. The pressure was constant, the pleasure exhausting.

Added to the hectic demands of drama school were the equally hectic demands of our social life. Falling in love was incredibly time- and tissue-consuming, and disentangling oneself even more so. But because we worked with each other so closely, a huge and comfortable safety net of friends developed. The Station pub in Sidcup was filled nightly with loud, witty drama students. Its toilets were filled with gossip and tears and planning. There were parties and "hops" and balls from which we'd weave our way home on secondhand bikes or red London buses, wearing miniskirts and the newly invented pantyhose, and singing "She's Leaving Home" from the Beatles' most recent L.P., *Sergeant Pepper's Lonely Hearts Club Band.* It was the height of the sixties. Carnaby Street beckoned and Mary Quant makeup plastered our faces. It was then that my hair became accustomed to changing its color at least five times a year. Vietnam was nowhere. Drug taking was not yet mandatory. Condoms were more common than the Pill, which was still in its infancy. Giddiness and happiness, love and peace, hope and opportunity—the world was ours.

Sidcup, where the college was situated, was half an hour by train from central London. I went to the theater often, more often than most of my friends since I'd been starved of it in "wildest" Africa. I saw John Gielgud in Chekhov's *Uncle Vanya*, scarcely able to believe that I was hearing his magnificent voice live and not on a 78 r.p.m. record reciting "Break, Break, Break." Peggy Ashcroft, Maggie Smith, Judi Dench, and Glenda Jackson were role models whom I watched and worshiped from the edge of my seat. I took the milk train early one Saturday morning to queue for standing-room-only at the Old Vic to see Laurence Olivier play *Othello*. When Othello made his entrance I recognized in him all the African men I'd ever known. His way of moving was so authentically *black* that I squinted in disbelief, peering forward to make sure that it was indeed Olivier and not an impostor.

These theatrical feasts raised my expectations as an actress and as a spectator. I knew what excellence was and grew impatient if it was absent. I'm now hard to please and rarely go to the theater. In Australia the voice and movement elements seem sloppy, as if being clear were unfashionable, but even in London I've been known to grumble, even about Shakespeare at the National Theatre.

Through our own acting, verse speaking, and storytelling

we were exposed to glorious literature, which we had to understand before we could speak it with meaning. The rigorous analysis of Shakespeare, for example, was essential for its believable interpretation. We came at literature from the hot angle, that is from the inside out, rather than the cold angle of academia, standing outside, aloof, gazing in. I gained useful different perspectives from each approach but preferred the uses for literature provided by drama school.

Hidden in the detours of my mind (I tried to forget them even as they occurred) are classes at drama school vaguely connected to teaching. They were exceptionally tedious. As yet unaware of the health hazard, we dragged on Player No. 6 cigarettes throughout all our Education lectures, clouding the room with so much smoke that we were able, if we were lucky, to lose sight of the boring man murmuring away at the front. Our real learning occurred in the schools on Practice Teaching. Few of us took an interest, but the course was so tightly disciplined that somehow we were force-fed the theory and practice we needed. We had plenty of "stuff" to teach. The meat of literature made up the meal of most lessons, but how to serve it up was left to trial and error. Most of us had a natural flair in the classroom. Teaching, we thought, was like having the main part in a one-person play in front of a trapped audience. It was years before I learned that good teaching meant being a producer-of-learning rather than being an actress-in-education. In shock I discovered that the *children* had to play the main parts, not I. Heavens, how it hurt.

Drama school cured me eventually of any desire to be an actress. I had arrived starving for acting, and had gorged myself on it. Towards the end of my third year my appetite had sickened and so died. Apart from the fact that my looks would forever prevent me from playing the part of Juliet but would instead assure me the part of Juliet's nurse, it was the times offstage that convinced me that an acting career would bore me to extinction. In the dressing rooms, alert for the next entrance, it was impossible to read a book or to switch off. Even when I had leading roles I chafed at the brittle, unproductive time spent in the wings. Gossip, for which I had developed a greedy appetite, began to pall in the tedium of its backstage repetition. Onstage, I dreaded acting yet again through other people's long speeches. It was only my own long speeches that I enjoyed.

Gradually I realized that what I really wanted was to be *known*. Being an actress as such wasn't important. I was uncertain as to how I'd achieve my shallow, but common, ambition. I thought it might be through radio, at which I'd excelled and which I adored. I was almost ashamed of having had such a splendid time wasting time for three years, but of course it wasn't wasted. I use the training every day of my life, particularly in my voice and speech: posh voice in posh shops, resonant voice for dull meetings, hushed voice in noisy classes, and musical voice for blind children. And then there's the expressive face for deaf children, the expressive hands for foreigners, the expressive arms for storytelling, and the expressive eyes for everything.

But the most important and lasting gift from drama school was the gift of language. What's the use of gesture or voice if one hasn't the language to be expressive *with*? Similarly, what's the use of a pen, or a little jar filled with sharpened pencils, if one hasn't the language to write *with*? I spent three years at drama school engrossed in learning how to act, being forced to learn how to teach, and accidentally learning how to write. My poor father, who had been so anxious about my training, was finally rewarded three times for the one course. The fact that it would take another fifteen years for the writer to write is neither here nor there.

The curtain is about to come down on these scenes from drama school, but there appears to be a star performer waiting in the wings.

5

Falling in Love Again . . . and Again

Some enchanted morning, when I saw the stranger across the crowded cafeteria, he looked French. There was an arrogant elegance about his style. I found out later that he was fluent in French, that he had spent a year teaching in France before coming to drama school, and that he would affect a French look forever, in spite of his acutely English character. In particular, I was to discover that the French look would manifest itself in the foppishness of his socks, which I would be called upon to admire for the rest of my life.

Malcolm Fox and Merrion Partridge were so entirely different in character, culture, and outlook that they would never have been drawn together in the normal run of events. However, in the staff room of a Hertfordshire teachers' college two women, one of whom knew my family and one of whom knew Malcolm's, happened upon the subject of drama schools. Such a coincidence! Both of them knew students at Rose Bruford's. Malcolm and I were invited for the weekend.

Malcolm's friends lived in a flat as National Trust caretakers of George Bernard Shaw's house at Ayot Saint Lawrence. A statue of Joan of Arc stood in the garden. In the house we rode Shaw's exercise bike; tried on his hats; pored over the photos of blown-up desert trains in an album belonging to Shaw's protégé, Lawrence of Arabia; marveled over the Augustus John line drawing of Lawrence on the mantelpiece; and hooted over the printed postcards on different subjects that Shaw would send to his correspondents. I slept in awe in Lawrence's bedroom.

So we were thrown together, Malcolm and I. We did not like each other. I found him brutally English. His coldness, his belief that *English* was a synonym for *good* and his snobbish attitude towards colonials—he actually called me a colonial!—repelled me. Besides, he was engaged to be married to a French girl, and if that wasn't reason enough to leave him alone, his outrageously theatrical mannerisms were.

We may not have liked each other, but both of us were similarly attracted by the magnet of travel. When Malcolm discovered I still had unused mileage on my air ticket from Rhodesia, he couldn't stand to see it wasted, which is how we came to spend a weekend in Paris in February 1966, with a friend of his called Mimi. She had a tiny flat, five floors

58

up, no lift. Accommodation was tight. I slept in a double bed. With Mimi. And Malcolm, in love with the city but not with me, introduced me to Paris.

While I was at Bruford's, holidays were awkward. I couldn't go home—it was too far and too expensive—and we had no relatives in England. My first Christmas with friends of the family was clouded by private howls of home-sickness in spite of the great kindness shown to me. After that, friends from college invited me home and I started to unravel the tight knitting of the English class system as I stayed with different families, like the miners in Derbyshire (D.H. Lawrence country), the farmers in Durham, and the stockbroking family in Surrey. I began to know the English and to love them for their honesty and kindness towards me.

My first summer holiday was spent in Israel. Many of my friends from school were Jewish—a third of Townsend High School had been Jewish—so I had some familiarity with the culture. In August '66, eager for cheap adventure of a trav-eling kind, I went on an organized student trip for five weeks to work on a kibbutz on the Lebanese-Israeli border: Kibbutz Manara. I climbed over the sagging barbed-wire fence once just to be able to tell Malcolm I'd been to Lebanon.

The work, picking plums and apples, was equally as tiring and as boring as picking cherries and strawberries had been the year before in Switzerland, but the weather was hotter and the people more cheerful and more easygoing. The group I went with was mostly Jewish. Having fun was uppermost in their minds. And mine. The fun died a bit when we were woken at 3:30 every morning to stagger bleary-eyed into the trucks that trundled us down to the apple orchards in the valley. We were silent going down and quiet as we stood like sleeping robots pulling apples off the branches. At 7:30 we stopped for a gigantic breakfast of fresh bread, yogurt, and fruit. After breakfast, because we'd been enlivened by the food, the orchards would be filled with singing, everything from Joan Baez songs to the national anthem of Israel. We also sang with relief all the way home for lunch at 11:30. The rest of the day, and the oppressive heat, was ours. Saturday, the Sabbath, was free. We would all greet each other on that day with *"Shabbat shalom."* On weekdays it was merely *"Shalom,"* meaning "Peace." Israel and its recent history came alive in conversations, in slide shows, in talks given by kibbutz staff, and in visits to frightening museums that preserved the horror of the Holocaust in the hope that it might never happen again.

But I learned about falling in love more than anything else by forming a passionate attachment with a young Moroccan, French-speaking Israeli. I hadn't known till then that there could be such a phenomenon as a Jewish Arab. When I wasn't working in the fields like Ruth, amid the alien corn, I spent my time with him. His name was Eli. He spoke Hebrew and French and I spoke French and English. My French improved almost to fluency. We decided to marry, although not immediately. When my work at the kibbutz came to an end, we visited different members of his family in Tel Aviv and Nazareth.

Nazareth, Jesus, God, the Bible. I was enchanted to find myself one morning walking—as custom had dictated in ancient times—behind Eli and his two male companions, beside a donkey, up a narrow lane. It seemed all right, in Nazareth. Then I was foolish enough to write to my mother about it and all Hell broke loose. Hadn't Jesus Christ tried

60

to liberate women in Nazareth itself two thousand years be-fore? Had I lost my senses entirely? What on earth did I think I was playing at? I was summoned home for Christmas. What jolted me back to reality, however, was attempting to communicate with Eli by letter. His written language was Hebrew. My written language was English. Our French, writ-ten down, killed the relationship.

Christmas was lovingly comfortable. I hadn't seen my family for almost two years, and sighed with relief to be home again. And there was the luxury of having a house girl to do my washing and ironing, although I felt guilty about that, remembering my time of servitude in Switzerland.

When I went back to drama school, in early '67, I dyed my hair ash blond. This small action had a great bearing on my future. Malcolm had decided to visit a school friend that April, Jill Lucas, who'd married an Egyptian and was living in Cairo. Malcolm had sufficient means for a respectable journey to Cairo by plane and train and boat, but none for his return. Hitching home would be necessary—and easier, he thought, with a blonde in tow. Would I go with him?

I went. My miniskirts and blond hair were embarrassingly unacceptable in Egypt. I had two scarves: one for my hair, and one to cover my knees whenever I sat down. Drama school was a taboo topic since acting and loose morals were inextricably entwined in the Egyptian ethos. One of Jill's wealthy relations offered Malcolm a great deal of money for me—I would be his third wife, he explained. We laughed until we realized he was serious. Jill provided us with fasci-nating insights into the Islamic world. For example, it was considered an extremity of wickedness to throw away bread. It had to be given away to the less fortunate, the man who removed the rubbish, for instance. Even crumbs were reverently collected from the floor. To have left them there would have been *haram*, a holy insult.

Middle Eastern food, deliciously interesting and healthy after the so-called food in England, gave Malcolm diarrhea and made me fat. When he recovered, we became shamefaced unoriginal tourists, right along the beaten track, riding on camels, watching belly dancers, climbing inside the Pyramids, and staring back at the Sphinx.

Together we rode the hot train south to Luxor and took a boat across the Nile. The barge we sat in was not a burnished throne, but Cleopatra's spirit hung heavily in the summer air. We rode bikes in the heat to the tomb of Tutankhamen in the Valley of Kings. When I was a child in Australia, I remembered, an English family had died in the desert between Adelaide and Birdsville because their car had broken down and they hadn't thought to carry water with them. Malcolm and I carried no water. We wore no hats. There were no trees to provide relief from the shimmering heat. I was the mad dog and Malcolm was the Englishman out in the noonday sun. We rode on, however, Tutankhamen beckoning. Panic was pointless. We had, after all, to ride all the way back as well. The grandeur of the Valley of Kings was lost in my thirst.

Later that day, when we'd gulped a lukewarm Fanta from a roadside stall, we pedaled onwards to the Colossus of Memnon. Being colossal myself at the time, and because of the "Mem," I felt a deep attachment to this monument. Both of us remembered the lines from "Ozymandias" and declaimed them across the empty fields in a shock of recognition:

Falling in Love Again . . . and Again

"I met a traveller from an antique land
Who said—'Two vast and trunkless legs of stone
Stand in the desert. . . .' "

Throughout this foreign excitement in Egypt's heat we remained cool, if not icy, towards each other. On the journey home we took a boat from Alexandria to Greece and hitchhiked all the way to the cross-Channel ferry in France, through Greece, Yugoslavia, Italy, and Switzerland. Six days of monosyllabic conversation.

In the Italian Alps our feet, clad in summer sandals from Cairo, froze in the snow. In Trieste, one midnight, we banged for hours on the door of a house that belonged to the great-uncle of a friend at drama school. "Visit him," she'd said. "He'd love you to stay." Our shouting and banging should have awakened the dead, but there was no answer. When we got back to England we found out he'd died. We spent that night on a pile of leaves in an Italian park. Penniless by now, we headed for Switzerland and the Château de Bossey to borrow money. The driver of the Mercedes who dropped us off gave us chocolate and apples when he discovered how hungry we were. Soon a hot bath and clean sheets transformed Bossey into heaven. The cleanliness, the tidiness, the ordered routine made me long to stay, but we pressed on the next day.

One night, later that week, cold and lost in the wet somewhere in France, we argued about something as trivial as not pronouncing the g in *Modigliani*, and sulked with our backs to each other in the rainy darkness. Shivering and miserable, we recovered sufficiently to tramp on until we arrived at what appeared to be a bus shelter, where Malcolm, to atone for his meanness, gave me his fat map of Italy to use as a mattress against the cold under my sleeping bag. In the morning we awoke to acres of sad little white crosses. We had slept beside war graves.

Our silence frosted further as we crossed the Channel. We read in a discarded newspaper an item about an injured seabird on the coast of England that had been rescued from a cliff by a helicopter, at enormous cost. I expressed the view that it had been a shocking waste of money. Malcolm gave me a withering Malcolm-look and said, "Well, you would think that, wouldn't you? How could you understand? You're not English."

On our return, during his final term at drama school, a wary intimacy developed between us, in spite of our differences. I thought it would be temporary. He went to France that summer to stay with the Other Woman. I went to Greece with Adrienne, a friend from drama school. My address was c/o American Express in Athens.

After weeks on the islands of Crete and Rhodes, Adrienne and I returned to Athens, mainly for the post. I disliked being out of touch with my parents for too long. When I gave my name and asked if there were any letters for me, the woman behind the counter laughed. "Partridge? Yes!" Beaming, she handed me a huge pile of post, including eight letters and twelve postcards from Malcolm. Dazed, I sat reading them on the stairs inside the American Express building and fell in love with the kind, warm, tasteful, friendly young Englishman who had had the very good sense to fall in love with me.

At the end of the summer he arranged to meet me in the middle of Westminster Bridge. He was carrying roses. It hasn't been roses all the way—the usual nettles have appeared now and then—but it was understood from that moment that we would eventually spend our lives together. My flatmate said it would never last because we were like chalk and cheese and would find it impossible to accommodate each other's personalities. Twenty-three years later we remember her inept warning and smile.

Malcolm had joined Voluntary Service Overseas (the British equivalent of Peace Corps) for two years. Two years! During my third year at drama school he taught in Tunisia, so of course I bought the cheapest ticket available and spent my April vacation with him. It was the idea of yet more travel as much as being with Malcolm that attracted me to Sfax, where he was living.

I made my final curtain call at drama school in July 1968. Suddenly I was at a loose end. Malcolm came home for the summer, which we spent with his parents in the little Lincolnshire village in which he'd grown up. His parents were nicer than Malcolm himself—my mother-in-law is the best in the world—so I stayed with them for weeks after he'd left for Africa, where he was to teach in the University of Rwanda for a year.

My future was uncharted. It had no map, no direction. I could teach and I could act, but I had no commitment to either. I lacked confidence as a teacher, having paid scant attention to that aspect of my training. Besides, my parents were both teachers, and it seemed unadventurous not to branch out. I also lacked the will to act. In England at any one time 80 percent of actresses are unemployed and, as I was no longer stagestruck, I felt no inclination to hang about waiting for the scraps of work that might or might not come my way. My first love was radio, but I had no idea of how to break into it.

Dimly, I assumed that Malcolm's career would be more important than mine and that he would eventually support me while I followed my lesser career (which career?) in between babies. Dimly, I assumed we would live in England. Dimly, I assumed we would buy a house, go shopping, see friends, and thus poddle along into an arthritic old age. I imagine that many women of my age at that time had similarly unexciting expectations, tentative self-esteem, and a timeless dependency on the opposite sex, in spite of their education.

In this dimness a single candle spluttered the possibility of a different future. In July 1968 as drama school came to an end I had made a brave entry in my journal: "I will write. . . . I WILL write." But even as I wrote it I guessed that success as a writer would be elusive and unlikely. I was whistling in the dark and I knew it.

In a panic, I fled England and went home to Rhodesia, hoping to find work—any work—for a year. My father, who had every right to say, "I told you so!," held his tongue. When no department stores or hotels would employ me, Dad paid me to teach on a voluntary basis at Jairos Jiri, a poverty-stricken center for disabled Africans. Teach? The horror, the horror.

To my surprise and dismay, teaching excited me. I cavorted through the term with my Standard Seven class, fitting in more drama than English composition (the subject I was supposed to be teaching), although I remember making a good fist of explaining how to connect paragraphs. The drama lessons were hampered by a pitiful lack of space and the fact that my adored students were in wheelchairs or on crutches, or blind. Radio, being one of my passions, seemed the ideal vehicle for my immobile class. At the end of the year we presented a Christmas "radio" program in which news was broadcast from Bethlehem, shepherds were interviewed in depth, advertisements for donkeys and camels were chanted and sung, and Mary sent in a request for a lullaby to hush the baby Jesus. All I can remember of the preparation for this performance is crying with laughter. Africans' sense of humor and their sense of timing, at least in my corner of Africa, are so perfect that even those children, whose lives were bleak and whose future was bleaker, were able to rock with laughter over their own spontaneous wit. I'm still in close contact with some of these, my first students, and a roll down memory lane is a must whenever we meet.

While I was at the Jairos Jiri school, a propagandist newspaper distributed on behalf of the racist Ian Smith regime found its way into each classroom. Storming with rage, I picked up the newspaper one morning and drew a tree on the blackboard. "See this tree?" I ranted. "It's the government! See this publication? It's a branch of the government—a poisonous branch of the government. It's full of lies. Lies, lies, lies! Do you understand?"

My father was disturbed by what I'd done. Informers, he told me, were everywhere. I had been foolish, and I wasn't to do it again. Later that week a police car appeared. It was being driven slowly as if those inside were looking for something, or someone. Guilt and fear made me think they were coming for me, and my first pointless impulse was to hide under the coffee table, but they drove on.

During these in-limbo months I applied for a position in

the Zambian Broadcasting Corporation. Zambia, Rhodesia's neighbor, was under black rule by then, and I felt I could live there with a clear conscience. When I got the job my self-concept soared. Not for me the humdrum life of an Ordinary Woman! Here was a Plan, a Career, a Future. Malcolm and I would live in Africa happily ever after. I was to start at the end of January 1969 and at the beginning of December Malcolm wrote from Rwanda to say that he'd scraped up the air fare and would be flying down for Christmas. It was too good an opportunity to miss. I decided, without being able to consult him, that we'd get married on January 2, in the middle of his two-week visit.

There was no time to tell Malcolm of these rushed arrangements for his future, although I knew he wouldn't mind. Letters to Rwanda went via Belgium and took weeks to arrive, since direct mail and phone contact with Rhodesia had been cut off by all the Black African states to the north. Making the plans without him knowing was hilariously exciting.

He was to fly to Zambia, where his best friend from school happened to be working, and together they were to drive down to Bulawayo, arriving on Christmas Eve. Early in the evening the phone rang. Malcolm had been stopped at the Rhodesian border and prevented from entering the country because he had no visible means of financial support. In other words he was broke. "But we're getting married in nine days' time," I wailed. He took the news well. I wrote down the phone number of the border post and said I'd ring back.

Well, I sobbed and bawled! My father, always calm in a crisis, sat on the verandah steps in the warm evening air. "Memzi," he said, "when I was in the air force in Darwin during the war we always went straight to the top in a crisis, so we'd better go straight to the top, eh?" My father, the miracle worker, tracked down the minister for immigration at a Christmas Eve party in the capital. He promised the minister he'd be Malcolm's guarantor. The minister rang the border post. We rang the border post. At four A.M. Malcolm, my Christmas present, rang the doorbell.

He had arrived, but how was he to return? He'd intended to borrow the money from Dad. The friends who gave us money as a wedding present never knew how we sat together laughing with relief, slowly adding it up until we had collected enough for his fare back to Rwanda. Since Paris in '66, we had been locked into a pattern of travel-on-the-cheap. Travel came first. How to pay for it came later. This is still the case.

The wedding was held in Hope Fountain church, and the place was packed, mostly with Africans. I was the only European ever to be married there. Two missionaries who'd known me since childhood tried to keep the service under control, but drama school turned the ceremony into a theatrical performance. I paused for so long between "for richer" and "for poorer" that my mother thought I was going to ignore "for poorer" altogether. I winked at Malcolm as I said it. We had his airfare. Did poverty matter? The Jairos Jiri kids grinned in the front pews. Barbara Bacon, the much-loved and more talented other half of the Barberrion singing duo of my youth, sang "One Hand, One Heart" from *West Side Story*, and African voices singing hymns gave our Rite of Passage the glorious grandeur I had longed for. Afterwards, in the heat outside, old African women sang high songs of celebration and stamped the dust in pounding rhythms, the seed pods and shoe-polish lids tied around their ankles making a joyful noise unto the hills.

"Wasn't it a great day?" I often say to Malcolm, and his patient reply is always the same: "I can't remember. I was too worried about my tapeworm." He'd arrived in Rhodesia infected with a tapeworm, which had made him exquisitely thin. (Malcolm, thin? What a sweet memory!) Our doctor had prescribed a violent medicine that would eventually cause the tapeworm to be evacuated in a rather spectacular bowel movement. So! His heartfelt vows had been a charade: the loo had been uppermost in his mind all the time.

On our wedding night a full moon rose into the sky. We stayed in my parents' tiny shack on a farm just beyond the African townships outside Bulawayo and went rowing on the nearby dam, in the moonlight. As we pulled on the oars the moon lit up one face, leaving the other in deep shadow. We shared this natural spotlight by turning the boat around, and around again, as water slapped against the oars and crickets chorused close by in the tall grasses. Then, as if by romantic design, drums began to beat in the distance, somewhere in the darkness of the African townships. Malcolm was impressed by my stage management of this scene. So was I.

A week later, he, bereft, left me, bereft, at the Bulawayo airport and flew back to Rwanda. My radio career in Zambia was due to start within three weeks. We would be apart for six solitary months. Or so we thought.

A week after Malcolm's return to Rwanda, one of his fellow volunteers resigned and hitched back to England, creating

70

a vacancy at the university that needed to be filled, urgently. Malcolm suggested that his wife—new word—might step into the breach.

I was torn between a career and a husband. To complicate matters, working in Rwanda meant *teaching* in Rwanda.

I taught in Rwanda. We began our married life with two servants, a cook, and a night watchman, so life at home was easy. The university was not in the capital, but in Butare, a town consisting of half a street. It was the most primitive country I'd experienced, and pathetically poor from over-population. In a mountain mission I saw children dying from kwashiorkor, the disease of malnutrition, their bellies huge but empty, their black hair turning brown and falling out. Merely to be clothed was to be wealthy, and guilt-ridden.

We were supposed to be teaching English, but in practice our students were drilled to learn by rote American English sentences about *corn flakes* and *movies* and *summer vacations in Colorado*, which had no relevance to their lives. Many had never even ridden in a car. The course was called English 900, and I remember its nine hundred sentences with shudders of shame. It was the antithesis of everything I knew about effective teaching. We argued for changes, but our American boss was adamant that not a full stop—sorry, period—or a comma could be changed.

As if this confinement weren't enough, he summoned us to his office and asked us not to call each other *darling* in public. Americans, he told us, used *darling* only in intimacy. How he could speak so confidently on behalf of 250 million people was a puzzle. We were furious. Some weeks later, when we were with him at a formal dinner, the British high commissioner (from neighboring Uganda), wishing to attract

71

the attention of his wife at the other end of a long table, called out, "Darling!" I could have kissed him.

In the April vacation, when we had been married for four months, two colleagues, Pauline, an American, and Rita, a Canadian, invited us to holiday with them in Uganda, touring the game parks by car. We had no money and no car. No choice. We accepted their invitation. I didn't really want to go. I wouldn't have gone if I hadn't been newly married. I don't like game parks. My African childhood had been full of holidays in game parks. My father would adjust and readjust the fiddly features on his camera as an evil rhino plodded down the narrow sandy road directly towards us while we kids lay trembling on the floor of the car, pleading, "Move, Dad! Move! Please!" The animals are wild, and game parks are dangerous. "Stay in your car and stay on the road," say the brochures. Sometimes Dad would drive off the road through the tall grass to get a better photo of a couple of lions lounging under a tree. It always made me shift with nervousness. I didn't want to go to the game parks in Uganda, but I went, just to be with Malcolm.

We went in Rita's car. It was a Peugeot, which pleased me. I like a reliable car in a game park. Rita and Pauline slept in five-star safari lodges each night, while we slept in the car and used their bathrooms in the morning. I woke up one night to feel the car rocking slightly. A hyena was scratching itself against the back bumper. I remember looking forward to the time when we might have enough money to book into Hiltons instead of sleeping in cars. At breakfast each morning, we mingled with the jet set from Europe and America who didn't know we'd slept in the car. We talked in accents that usually imply at least an aristocratic background if not vast sums in Zurich. Thank God for drama school.

We drove through all the game parks. The other three were like babies in their naive expressions of excitement and wonder at every animal they saw. As for me! Giraffes were a yawn, warthogs were a bore, zebras were dull, crocodiles were frightening, elephants were frightening, lions were frightening, and thundering herds of buffalo were frightening. I was happy because I was newly married. Malcolm and I held hands in the backseat except when he was taking photos. The others were never frightened because they didn't understand the danger. That is, they weren't frightened until after the elephant.

On the particular day in question the car had already broken down once beside a herd of zebra. Malcolm, who knew nothing about cars and still doesn't, had leaped out and opened the bonnet. Rita, who knew everything about cars, had connected two wires that had come apart. They'd both climbed into the car in less than a minute and we had driven on. In the late afternoon we came upon a herd of elephants. There were baby elephants in the herd. Like kittens and puppies, they were overwhelmingly adorable.

We drove slowly past the herd and stopped some distance away so that the three doting tourists I was traveling with could take photos. When the click-clicking had come to a stop, Rita turned the key to start the car. Nothing. She turned it again. Nothing. It was completely dead. We knew that the two wires had merely to be reconnected for the car to be able to start, but we knew, too, that while the elephants were so close it would be dangerous to get out.

So we just sat there. At least when my father stopped in

73

game parks he used to leave the engine running. We just sat there. The elephants went on grazing.

After a minute or two we decided in whispers to close the windows so that the elephants wouldn't be disturbed by our scent. Five minutes passed. It was too long. A female elephant moved away from the herd. She mistrusted us. We were a threat to her babies. I saw her move onto the road and turn towards the car. Her trunk moved suspiciously through the air and her great ears flapped angrily against her shoulders. When she began to paw the dusty road behind us, I lay down on the floor of the car and pulled a coat over my head. I dreaded the shadow that would fall over the car before she trampled it. I put my fingers in my ears and squeezed my eyes tightly shut. None of us moved. We scarcely breathed.

Eventually, I asked Malcolm, in whispers, what was happening. In the prison of his fear his voice came out like a detached BBC commentator. I nearly laughed. "Well, I'm sorry, darling. The elephant does seem to be coming towards us at a fairly rapid rate. It is, actually, making directly for us. It's angry. Its ears are flapping. It's coming." I sank back under the coat. I was appalled at the possible pain of dying. I imagined a great foot lifted above the car, coming down, crushing the top of the car onto us, breaking us into pieces, grinding us into the ground. I heard my heart beating in my temples and decided to pray. It was clear that only a miracle would save us. "Dear God," I said, "if You let me live I'll do anything You like. I promise to be useful. I promise to be tolerant. I promise to be generous. Just let me live." (My mother had been asking me for years to be useful, tolerant, and generous.) I then tried to imagine the headlines in the newspapers: "Tragic End for Newlyweds." I didn't like that one. "Newlyweds Trampled by Elephants" didn't sound much better. I decided to peep out.

The shadow of the elephant had fallen across the car. Malcolm was yellow with fright. Rita, who was very fat, had massive drops of sweat on her upper lip. The hair on her forehead was sopping. Pauline was so white and still that she looked dead. The elephant had lumbered rapidly towards the car and halted at the last minute. It ambled around the car. And slowly again, around the car. And again. Inside the car we were ready to explode with suspense. Our fear seemed audible. Twenty-five minutes! It was twenty-five ages before that elephant felt sure enough of our innocence to wander back to its herd. Gradually the herd moved away. Malcolm and Rita crawled out of the car, opened the bonnet very gently, reconnected the wires, and eased themselves back into the car. Rita's wonderful fat fingers turned the key and the whole world burst into the music of a car engine that worked.

We survived the holiday, returned to Rwanda, and once again contemplated our future. Our lives were at a crossroads without signposts.

"How about Australia?" I ventured.

"Australia!" said Malcolm. "It's on the other side of the world. And anyway we couldn't scrape up the fare."

I told him how English migrants were being encouraged to settle in Australia. "They're called ten-pound migrants, Malcolm. They want migrants so badly they're charging them only ten pounds for their outward passage. It would cost us

75

twenty pounds and we'd only have to stay two years. Besides, there's Granddad aged ninety and all alone in Adelaide. He's been good to me and I'd like to be good to him."

I knew that the words *colony* and *colonial* were hovering around Malcolm's English lips, but he had the grace not to utter them. The cheapness of the fare was irresistible, *colony* notwithstanding.

We wrote to the authorities in England. A question mark hung over my Australian passport: Could an Australian become an Australian migrant? The decision came down in my favor since I'd been an expatriate most of my life. We would have to spend six months in England in order to qualify for our assisted passage.

Back to London we went. Malcolm taught in Dalston Junction in London's East End. I worked in the West End in a dusty warehouse off Oxford Street packing ribbons and belts for export, freezing in miniskirts, wheezing asthmatically in our damp flat in Clapton Pond. (Asthma is a chronic fact of my life.) I had not dared to teach in London. I never wanted to teach again. Instead I dreamed of a bright future in Australia working for ABC radio, preferably in education. Heavens, I thought, they'll be so pleased to employ someone with my talent, experience, and qualifications.

My life in London was so unremarkable that the negative highlight of those months in waiting was being sexually harassed on the London underground. I traveled with millions of others every morning and evening in a silent stupor of dull routine, packed tight against the bodies of strangers, locked into face-to-face positions with an alarming variety of the human race. One morning I felt something traveling up the inside of my leg. At first I wasn't concerned. In the crush, errant umbrellas were often forced into awkward positions involuntarily. When the "thing" stopped traveling and started stroking, I averted my eyes from the greasy face directly in front of me, to push away whatever it was. A clammy hand met mine.

How could this man whose face was inches away dare to do what he was doing? I was not my mother's daughter for nothing. As we tumbled out at Oxford Street I ran after him, shrieking, "You bastard!" The silent, circumspect commuters hunched themselves more deeply into their indifference. I caught up with my aggressor and walloped him so hard across the shoulders that he staggered and almost fell. "You creep! You dirty old man!" I screamed, still in pursuit. Adrenaline gave strength to my anger as I delivered another mighty blow to his back. Satisfied but hysterical, I burst into tears and traveled sobbing up the escalator, ignored by everyone around me.

Malcolm, to whom I told the story that evening, was inordinately proud of my behavior. Now, whenever the subject of sexual harassment arises, he leaps in with, "Mem bashed up a man on the tube once," and then waits for me to retell the story of my Amazonian heroism.

I had had enough of London. The food, the filth, the poverty, and the cold had ground me down. The understanding woman who arranged our air tickets to Australia asked us when we'd like to leave.

"January the second," said Malcolm. "Our first wedding anniversary."

He forbore to tell her that we realized champagne would be cheaper on the plane. Because we were teachers, and therefore in demand (those were the days!), our baggage allowance was increased from forty-four to eighty-eight pounds each. When the Qantas pilot said, "G'day, ladies and gentlemen," I nearly wept and Malcolm forgot to say *colonial*.

We arrived in Australia on January 4, 1970. Only for two years, mind you.

6

Welcome Home,
Merrion!

Sydney was just as it should have been when we arrived: steamy, with blue skies. Out of the plane, pale, bleary-eyed migrants stumbled gratefully into the heat and the future, Malcolm and I among them. As usual, building works were in progress at the Sydney airport, so we entered Australia via a hangar in which we stood sweating in eager queues. I felt personally responsible for Australia and hoped it would behave nicely as I introduced it to my wary husband.

As I handed over my passport the immigration official looked over the top of his glasses and asked why I was coming in as a migrant when my passport showed I was Australian.

I explained that I'd been an expatriate and now wanted to return to life in Australia permanently. He gave me the friendliest smile and said, "Welcome home, Merrion!" The amazement on Malcolm's face indicated that this behavior, while terribly un-British, nevertheless had a certain native charm.

In Adelaide we were welcomed again, this time by a friendly and well-meaning member of the Good Neighbour Council whose job it was to make migrants feel comfortable during their first few weeks. Malcolm found the friendliness appalling. He wanted to ease into the culture in his own guarded way, in his own time. Instead his English reserve was totally ignored by friendly Australians who didn't recognize reserve even when it was frosting the air before their faces.

We were driven to our migrant hostel by an employee of the National Bank, with whom we'd signed up in England. And this on a Sunday morning! At the migrant hostel for young married couples (actually an old house in Parkside, not one of the Nissen huts to which families were sent) the proprietor welcomed us warmly yet again with a casual take-it-or-leave-it friendliness.

We took the tram into the city on our second day and walked down King William Street from Victoria Square to Parliament House. It was only a few blocks. "Where's the rest of it?" asked Malcolm. There was no "rest of it." King William Street was it. In the months and years to follow, when we marched against the Vietnam War and against apartheid in South Africa the route from Victoria Square to Parliament House detoured down the major streets off King William Street in order to make the protest longer and somehow more worth the effort. In one of those marches, for the first and last time in my life I was spat upon by a woman who stood on the pavement screaming abuse at the protestors as we marched past.

We had been prepared for this abuse in our first week when we went to the cinema and found to our amazement that "God Save the Queen" was being played prior to the start of the film. We did not stand. No one in England would have stood in a cinema for "God Save the Queen." In Adelaide everyone stood, except us. When the elderly couple next to us sat down again one hissed to the other, "Communists!"

"Do we have to stay two years?" Malcolm whispered. Fortunately, the Dunstan decade and the Whitlam years were not far off. (Don Dunstan was an innovative and very liberal premier of South Australia. Gough Whitlam, our prime minister in the seventies, was to Australia what President Kennedy was to America: a refreshing, charismatic, liberal, and inspirational leader.)

Our main reason for choosing Adelaide of all Australian cities was my grandfather—he of the generous heart who had made drama school possible. He was ninety when we arrived, and lived in an old people's home in North Adelaide that became the setting and provided the characters for my book *Wilfrid Gordon McDonald Partridge*. (Granddad was also Wilfrid Partridge, like his son.) Although he was stooped and had a long white beard that caused children to ask him if he were Father Christmas, he walked so briskly around the park in nearby Wellington Square that I had to do a little skip every now and then to keep up with him.

Getting to know him was a treat. He subscribed to the

81

Times Literary Supplement, sat in the sun sewing exquisite tapestries, wrote essays on the impossibility of the Virgin Birth, played patience, pored over the shares index in the *Advertiser* ("Never sell, Mem, buy!"), told me about the past and his war (1914–18), and in the last month of his life wrote to the prime minister, Malcolm Fraser, telling him how to run the country.

I visited him every weekend, grateful that our relationship had been able to develop even though it was only for the last six years of his life. When, finally, he caught pneumonia, he sank rapidly and died within two weeks. In those weeks he often seemed dead already, breathing terribly, then not breathing at all. Once in panic during a silence I shook him alive. "Granddad! Granddad, please." Dazed, he murmured. He was not a demonstrative man, but the nurse in charge said, "Hold his hand. He does know someone's here, even if he doesn't know it's you. It will give him comfort." So I held his hand. My book *Sophie* arose directly from the throat-seizing sadness of this scene.

It was once pointed out to me that many of my books are about relationships between the young and the old: *Wilfrid, Sophie, Shoes from Grandpa, Night Noises, Guess What?, With Love at Christmas,* and even *Possum Magic.* I was asked why this was so and could only conclude that it must have had some connection to my friendship with Granddad. Relating to grandparents is uniquely different from relating to parents, husbands, or children. With grandparents the tone of the bond is almost conspiratorial. I tried to catch that essence of conspiracy in Wilfrid's relationship to Miss Nancy: "He called her Miss Nancy and told her all his secrets"; and in Emily's relationship to Lily Laceby in *Night Noises:*

"Are you really ninety?" whispered Emily, aged four and a half. Lily Laceby held her hand and smiled. "Inside I'm only four and a half like you," she said, "but don't tell anyone!"

Beverly Cleary, the writer of the much-loved Ramona series and other books, once said: "If you lacked something as a child, give it to yourself in a story." I think that's exactly what I've done. I've given myself grandparents over and over again.

In the Nature versus Nurture debate my grandfather always came down on the side of nature. Because my fingernails were like his, it followed that everything must be hereditary: my love of teaching from my father, my radical (in his eyes) politics from my grandmother, and my loud personality from my mother. He's the one who'd been a journalist, so had he lived to see me publish *Possum Magic*—how I wish he had!—he would have pooh-poohed it as "hereditary, Mem, merely hereditary."

Between visiting Granddad, being hissed in the cinema, and setting up home in a bald little flat that we thought was heaven because it had a bathroom that didn't require a shilling in the hot-water meter before we took a shower, we looked for work. A friend of my family, Bronte Bunney, sent Malcolm Fox to Hedley Beare (the names were incredible) in the Education Department. Within ten days of arriving, Malcolm had a job, a full-time teaching position in a boys' technical high school teaching English. No French. No drama. But a salary, nevertheless: $3,700 per annum.

As planned, I floated off to the ABC one hot morning, dramatically dressed and sporting a large white summer hat with a floppy brim. I felt like an actress. I looked like an actress. I would be an actress, on radio. It was not an auspicious start: the ABC was housed in a tattered old building in tired old Hurtle Square in the middle of town. In spite of my brightly explaining who I was and all about my training and experience, the ABC was as coolly uninterested as if I'd been a stray cat who'd wandered in from the nearest dustbin. "We don't employ actresses full-time. The few plays we produce are acted by talented amateurs who've been on our books for years. We have enough announcers, thank you. You want work in education? Perhaps we could find you something. No university degree? Great Scott! Then of course we can't employ you. Good day."

I had been so quaintly confident that the colony of Australia would gratefully receive my straight-from-England talent that when it didn't I was irrevocably crushed. Instead of fighting back and persisting, I gave up. I hadn't thought of any career other than the ABC, so when it fell through I fell apart. Money was tight. I needed work. Through the Federal Department of Education and Science I took on, unhappily, the one-to-one teaching of English as a foreign language to students from Pakistan, Laos, Iran, and the Solomon Islands for six hours a week.

The ABC gave me the odd part in the odd radio play. I remember best Henry James's *Daisy Miller* because I had the leading role. But it was intermittent work and badly paid. In early February, during a rehearsal at the ABC, the director of the play I was in called me aside and said, "I hear you can teach drama."

"Yes, I can," I said briskly, "but I never intend to."

"I was wondering if you could help my wife out of a

corner, actually. She's been employed by a Catholic girls' school for two and a half days a week. Grade Three through to Matric. She was due to start on Tuesday, but she's had to go into hospital for a major operation." Reluctantly I agreed to fill in. Temporarily.

His wife did not recover sufficiently quickly to want her job back. Unwittingly I had been tricked into the long-dreaded teaching career. Two days after my chat with the ABC director I taught eight lessons straight, at Cabra Dominican College, where I remained for the rest of 1970. Teaching was an incredible thrill. As well as my usual hand-bag-and-books baggage I took everything that made me tick as a person into the classroom, never role-playing the teacher, always being frankly myself. I was rapped over the knuckles once for talking about birth control. Energy and adrenaline pumped through me wildly in every class. Past students whom I meet now claim I either radicalized or scandalized every student I taught.

I had never come across Catholics before and treated them much like a Venezuelan might treat a Norwegian—as completely foreign. They turned out, however, to be human, even the nuns who were still in their long black-and-white habits. When I was seven months pregnant and rehearsing 120 Year Tens in an end-of-year show, an elderly nun came in to watch.

"Girls, girls!" she said. "A chair for Mrs. Fox!"

"It's all right, Sister," I said. "You'll make me feel like a queen."

"But my dear, you are a queen. A queen among women." And all because I was pregnant!

Through the Catholic system I found more work teaching

drama from Grade One to Grade Four at a parish school divinely named Our Lady of Fatima. Three jobs. But not a lot of money.

Malcolm, the man, was of course fully employed. I, the woman, listened to housewives' radio as I did the ironing on my spare afternoons in the flat, with a kitten called Theo for company. (Theo Tucker had taught us ballet at drama school.) Theo the kitten reminded me of my broken career, the promises of fulfillment dispersing into the air with the steam from the iron. I was vaguely disappointed rather than angry. Anger belongs to feminists, and I was not sufficiently aware to be a feminist. My lot, as an ironer of shirts, was so predictable that I was not surprised by it. I accepted it as being the way things were.

In the domestic atmosphere that prevailed we decided in March to have a baby. It seemed like a good idea. Fun. Interesting. In our lives every Rite of Passage had to become a major theatrical ritual, so we cut my last remaining packet of the Pill into lots of tiny gold squares and threw them over our heads like confetti.

I knew I was six weeks pregnant halfway through July. The next day the world knew. Cabra girls from the class of 1970 remember the impact twenty years later. How pleased I was. How overjoyed Malcolm was. How thrilled we are still, with Chloë.

7

A Motherhood
Statement

At Chloë's request this chapter is short—"Well, how
would you like being written about at my age?"—and therefore entirely out of proportion to the importance of motherhood in my life. Ah, well. Needs must.

We did everything right. From the moment we knew I
was pregnant we were happy—wildly happy, so that she'd
be happy in the womb. And I ate all the right foods to make
her healthy. And played loud music to keep her entertained.
And rested to keep her calm. And exercised to make her
strong. Oh, yes! Before Chloë was born I was the perfect
mother.

As she was born, I sang the Beatles' "Penny Lane," which I'd rehearsed for weeks beforehand, having read that singing during childbirth helped women not to scream. It was marginally helpful, as entertainment for startled nurses if nothing else. Nevertheless, the pain was outrageous. Halfway through I leaned up on one elbow and said to Malcolm, "This is the last time, my darling. I'm never doing this again." I panted through it like a pet dog, remembering my prenatal instructions precisely. Later, a nurse patted me on the head, making me feel even more like a pet dog, and said, "Your pants were perfect," as if I could have cared less. I was now A Mother.

My first words to Chloë as I cradled her in my inexpert arms were, "Hello, my darling." Malcolm cried—and he's an Englishman. Our child was perfect, of course, since perfection is in the eye of the beholder. A shock of black hair stood like exclamation marks around her head. Her eyes were huge and blue. Her tiny little bottom fitted perfectly into the palm of my hand. She was all things bright and beautiful.

I walked her up and down my room at the Queen Victoria Hospital, introducing myself rather nervously, explaining the world and how it worked.

"You're Chloë," I said, "and I'm your mother. Mothers love babies, that's why they have them. I'm going to be the best mother in the whole wide world!"

Of course I wasn't. Of course I'm not. There have been times when I've been such a Bad Angry Mother that I've chosen not to remember that her tiny bottom once fitted perfectly into the palm of my hand. Evidence of my volatility—and hers, since it was she who maddened me in the first place—can still be seen in the splintered dent in Chloë's bedroom door where I kicked it. The kitchen floor is chipped in three places from a tantrum in which I flung her special mug to the floor, breaking it into a thousand pieces while she, aged twelve, sobbed, "My mug. My baby mug. My mug." I haven't forgiven myself for that one. Fortunately, the mandarin orange that flattened on impact with the dining-room floor when I once went wild with rage and threw it down with all my might, has long since been scraped up and laid to rest in the compost heap. Chloë and I have driven each other screaming wild on many an occasion. I am not a perfect mother. And she's not a perfect child. Well, not quite.

At the age of three she cracked her first joke and was mighty pleased when I hugged her and shouted with laughter. She's never looked back. We were shopping when she asked me what *super* meant. "Fantastic," I said. "So," said Chloë, "next time you go to the petrol station you can say, 'Fill 'er up with fantastic, please!' "

We read aloud to her until at five and a half she said, "I can read faster by myself," since when she has never stopped. From *Fourth Term at St. Clare's* to Margaret Mahy, *Cosmopolitan*, *Hollywood Wives*, Dickens, *Charlotte's Web* (in French), Tom Sharpe, and David Lodge—she's read them all. In a house full of books, four of which she is often reading simultaneously, her common cry is, "There's nothing to read in this house." I once recommended Steinbeck's *East of Eden* so strongly that I put her off it for life. Occasionally she remembers it and says, "There's nothing to read in this house except some dumb Steinbeck a madwoman recommended years ago, and I'm not reading *that!*"

Until she was seven I sang to her every night, sweet and low, stealing away with Barbara Allen to the Red River

Valley and the Swanee River, wishing her *guten Abend* and *gute Nacht,* and letting her know that she was the cream in my coffee, she was the lace in my shoe. I was nuts about her. Still am, I guess.

Until she was well into high school I knelt nightly at her bedside, my elbows on the bed and my chin in my hands in an attitude of idolatry, talking to her about life, reflecting on big issues like school, smoking, love, sexism, employment, and the future, which I always expected to be bright, in her case. (It has so far lived up to my expectations.) In the dark, as we chatted, I could feel her values developing, preparing her, I hoped, for whatever lay ahead. She wanted me to be beside her, to clutch her hand, to make the world safe. I was glad to be there as "the mother."

I'm still glad to be there, so long as Malcolm's there too, sharing the highs and lows of parenthood. My positive view of motherhood owes much to him, since I'm often able to be a part-time mother, as it were. I escape from the constancy of mothering through the extensive travel associated with my work, safe in the knowledge that he and Chloë will have a fine time without me. But even when the responsibility of motherhood does slow down my days and cut off some of my choices, I like being a mother. The choices that remain are more than enough compensation. I love being around Chloë, listening to her exaggerating the anecdotes of her life to make me laugh. I love her loudness bursting through the mundaneness of an ordinary day. I feel especially important when she's ill or upset, because I'm needed, but I also like watching her detaching herself from me as she grows older, because I'm not needed. I also feel important when I'm ill or upset, and she tucks me up with her ragged Bed Rabbit and reads me "Eeyore's Birthday" from *Winnie-the-Pooh* in the same mournful tones I used to use when she was little.

How could I not like being a mother? It's provided such a wealth of happiness and laughter and memories. Even during the ghastliness of Where-did-I-go-wrong? arguments when she and I both turn into monsters, I like being a mother. It's a very dramatic, demanding role, and the script is almost impossible to get right, but still I like the part. Heavens, I don't "like" it—I'm being too cowardly to admit to my true feelings, as if loving one's child were embarrassingly unfashionable: I adore Chloë and I love being a mother!

Here endeth my motherhood statement.

8

For Poorer

A stray glance of Malcolm's fettered us to Australia by setting in motion a series of events that made us the victims of circumstance. One thing led to another until we realized, after Chloë was born, that Australia wasn't an adventure at all: it was home.

In 1970, when Malcolm was working full-time, he'd found out, by catching sight of a colleague's paycheck, that first-year-out teachers with university degrees were being paid more than he was. It upset him. Not the money so much as the idea that his competence and experience were being undervalued.

Spurred into action, he made immediate enquiries about enrolling for a B.A. in drama, French, and Italian at Flinders University, a new and exciting institution that happened also to be an energetic hotbed of student unrest at the time. In March 1971, when Chloë was three weeks old, he embarked on four years of study that he reveled in, and from which he emerged with a first-class honors degree in French in 1974. To keep the wolf from the Foxes' door, he took over my half-time drama job at Cabra and also taught English as a second language for a couple of hours a week.

We were poor. Food, electricity, and phone bills were a nightmare and Chloë's clothes were bought from Central Methodist Mission shops. We couldn't live on what Malcolm earned.

When Chloë was six weeks old, the Department of Education and Science arranged for me to teach English to a Ph.D. student from Iran, Acram Taji. For a couple of hours each day over five months, I was entertained and stimulated by my amusing and brilliant student, and earning enough to pay the rent. (We'd moved into a little house just before Chloë was born.) Just at the time when I might have been most despondent about being at home with a baby, surrounded by the pieces of my broken career, Acram provided a lively release from my otherwise suburban existence.

I had the best of both worlds: a child and a job that didn't take me from her. But it didn't last, because Acram learned English and went off to do her studies. From September 1971 until the end of 1972 I taught English to migrants part-time at the Institute of Technology in Adelaide, and had to find someone to take care of Chloë. I felt, in my overprotective way, that a child-care center would be too

93

hectic and impersonal for her, so we hired a child-care nurse and later a lovable grandmother whose own grandchildren lived elsewhere.

In spite of our part-time jobs we were often miserably short of money. I remember, after one two A.M. feed, tucking Chloë in and then going into the kitchen and sobbing against the fridge in despair over our finances. I had been an asthmatic-under-control since I was thirteen, but anxieties of 1971–72 hospitalized me with asthma three times. On one occasion I had turned blue even before I was wheeled into Casualty, and turned bluer as a young doctor, panicking, tried to find a vein for the drip. Another doctor was called, and I lived. I now take three drugs regularly and daily for asthma and it has decided, mostly, to leave me alone.

Malcolm was a super-dad, not only when I was in hospital. His hours at work and at university were irregular enough for him to spend almost as much time with Chloë as I did: the role of absent-father-at-work was never his. When I was ill, Malcolm's university lecturers and the nuns and other staff at Cabra were most understanding. He would take Chloë to all his classes. At Cabra the girls would take it in turns to mind her and at the university she played quietly with blocks under the lecturers' desks.

We doted on our gorgeous little kid, partly because she was so attractively happy and interesting, and partly because we had both the time to enjoy her and the time to get away from her. Our outside-the-home fulfillment meant that we had no reason to regret our sudden decision to become parents: Chloë hadn't wrecked our lives. On the contrary, she was great entertainment. We clapped and laughed at and kissed her every achievement. Thus began a cycle of achievement equals praise, equals a desire for further achievement, equals more praise, and so on. The ritual continues, even though she's now twenty.

Malcolm was due to finish his studies by the time Chloë turned four. For financial reasons we decided not to have a second child until then, but by then, 1975, we'd become too accustomed to the ease of an only child to want to disturb Chloë's equilibrium or my newly developing career. The decision was put off again and again. Our only child had never been intended by us to be "only," in spite of my "Never again!" protestation as Chloë was being born. It just turned out that way.

At the end of 1972 an advertisement appeared in the *Advertiser* for a tutorship in drama at Sturt Teachers' College. Malcolm urged me to apply. I urged him to apply. But he wanted to get his B.A. first, he said, and he had another two years to go (by which time the drama jobs in tertiary institutions had dried up completely and he would have to wait thirteen years before another was advertised).

I lacked the confidence to apply, so Malcolm impatiently wrote out an application and said, "Sign it! You can do this job standing on your head. You went to Rose Bruford's! And you're a natural teacher. I can't understand what you're so nervous about. Sign!"

So I signed. And I started work at Sturt College full-time in February 1973. I wasn't quite twenty-seven. Terrified that I wouldn't succeed, I dressed dramatically in floor-length Laura Ashley dresses, bought in anticipation of my new salary of just over four thousand dollars per annum, and role-played being a drama tutor, sweeping into this class and floating into that much as Rose Bruford had done when I'd been a student.

The work was tailor-made for me and I for it. Within days I had developed a craving for the adrenaline of teaching. I was potty about my students. Had anyone, I asked myself, ever been so exquisitely contented? Ever been so fortunate? Ever been paid for having such a good time? Surely not. Which is why I'm still here, still being rewarded, eighteen years later.

9

Mending My Broken Career

Malcolm has taken part in the drama of my life either as a costar or stage manager for over twenty years. He's supported me through every scene, applauding my characterization in each new role: wife, mother, teacher, student, and writer. And if he's faded from the spotlight of my story now and then, it's only because he's been busy behind the scenes making sure the show goes on.

I mention Malcolm because he and my father are such exceptional people that I tend to view all men in a sympathetic light, most of the time. For this reason neither the study of feminism nor being a feminist has ever held much interest for me, since I rarely feel that I've suffered from having been born a woman. However, I realize I belong to a privileged minority of the female kind, so I've never been antifeminist. I know that there are millions of women in need of a variety of liberations: legislative, work-related, social, biological, financial, educational, and personal, and I applaud those who work on their behalf.

Once, in 1972, I briefly joined a women's liberation group because I'd been rattled by Germaine Greer's *Female Eunuch.* But the sisterhood didn't accept me. Nor did I accept it. I was out of tune at the time, anachronistic, as an ecstatic mother and an unharmed wife. I went to two meetings. The movement, I discovered, was only for those women who were "ideologically sound." Being unsound and uncomfortable, I turned my back and walked away. When I left my particular sisterhood I imagine those who remained sighed with relief, but I was distressed about my departure since I too was a woman and a sister, but had been made to feel as alien as a brother.

By the mid-seventies I was beginning to believe that I'd be able to ignore my womanhood, at least in the workplace. If I worked hard and successfully, I said to myself, I'd be rewarded as a person whose sex was irrelevant. My naiveté belonged to a fairy story far removed from the reality of my story at the South Australian College of Advanced Education.

When I was employed in 1973 as a tutor in drama at the Sturt campus I was earning three dollars less per week than the college cleaners. Did I mind? Of course not. As a woman conditioned into thanksgiving for the crumbs of a career from the men's breadloaf, I was thrilled to have a job at all.

My one-year contract didn't bother me either. I threw myself vigorously and conscientiously into my work, loved teaching, and was stimulated by my students. The following year I was rewarded with another one-year contract. Oh, the joy of it! To be employed, yet again. I developed new courses. My workload increased as demand for my courses grew. I knew what I was talking about and I taught well, although it seems rather *de trop* to say so in such a bald fashion. My efforts were appreciated by the college and by my students. My workload grew. I was given another one-year contract, still at the tutorship level, for which I was humbly appreciative.

I persuaded myself that I didn't mind the pay, nor the conditions, since the rewards of being at the college were intrinsic to my teaching. I couldn't mind. I didn't dare to mind. Tutors on contracts, whether they're male or female, are pliable slaves, willing to take on whatever is necessary to ensure a contract the following year. Women in particular, in their excessive gratitude for employment, are the most compliant slaves of all. And so it was that at the end of three years I was offered yet another one-year contract at tutorship level.

By this time I was beginning to be able to hear the chains of my exploitation rattling. Tutors were not supposed to give lectures. I did. Tutors were not supposed to coordinate courses. I did. I received sympathy, but no action. I grumbled gently. There were members of staff teaching ten hours a week whose salaries were more than twice my own although my weekly contact hours hovered at around twenty-six. I complained politely and was rewarded with a three-year contract at tutor level for which I was again idiotically grateful, until I realized that seven years as a tutor on contract was to be a college record.

At home I stormed and wept, enraged over my conditions. At work a stressful bitterness soured my days, even though I knew that my own lack of assertion was a major cause of my unhappy situation. My despair knew no bounds when I discovered that in my case tenure had been dismissed without serious consideration when someone in a meeting had said, "Mem's going to have another baby, isn't she? She doesn't need tenure."

My agitation for promotion and permanency raged on for over two years. I was finally granted tenure at the beginning of 1980 and promoted to the still-lowly level of lecturer III, for which yet again I was grateful. In my experience women need constant reassurance that they have unreservedly deserved promotion. Men, in contrast, regard it as a right. I apportion no blame to either sex for its respective attitudes since blame is inappropriate in the circumstances, but it does make me wonder wistfully how weird it would be to have been born a man, and to have been conditioned into what appears to be such unshakable arrogance.

Between 1980 and 1986 the desert of my career bloomed. My papers were published in reputable journals. My presence and presentations were requested at major conferences around Australia as well as in Sweden, England, and the U.S.A. In a climate hot with excitement over the teaching of writing, I was able to offer a rare view: that of a writer who understood intimately the process of writing, together with that of a teacher who understood current research into the teaching of it. This fortuitous and simultaneous wearing of two hats gave my work a dynamic perspective, in which theory met practice and practice refined theory almost daily.

I was successful, but my success didn't bequeath me that badly needed, elusive male quality of being able to believe in my own worth. I remained diffident about my abilities, unsatisfied with my practice, unsettled by my reflections. Slowly I climbed the incremental ladder.

In 1986 the guidelines for promotion to senior lecturer in my institution changed dramatically. The Staff Association and the equal opportunities officer, believing that social brakes had been applied to women's advancement, listed new criteria for promotion, the most important of which was a proven ability to teach.

I was mildly encouraged by this news since teaching had always been one of my strengths, but as I still wasn't on the top scale, let alone on the top rung of that scale, and wouldn't be reaching such a step for another six years, I thought the new criteria would have no immediate impact on my life. I was tremendously busy as a lecturer and as a writer at that time and almost missed the apocalyptic news that anyone, on any scale, could apply. Still, I was a woman and felt it might be an effrontery to attempt such a climb from where I currently stood.

The union took me aside and explained that it had been precisely for people like me that the new guidelines had been introduced. Would I please apply? Tentatively I agreed that I would if I could find the time to write a sufficiently careful application. At the end of June 1986 I lodged my huge and hopeful application, shuddering at my audacity. Eighty-one other lecturers had done the same, in the hope that one of the seven available senior lectureships would be theirs. Many had applied for the umpteenth time.

Towards the end of November the campus dean phoned me in my office to ask if he could have a word in private. I dreaded his knock. When I opened my office door his face was serious. He told me to sit down. I'd been promoted to the position of senior lecturer in my first application, leaping seven incremental steps. I'd made history and he wanted to be the first to offer his congratulations.

Throughout this saga, anecdotal and documentary evidence supported my hunch that I wasn't alone among women in having been denied recognition in this manner. There are many cases like mine across Australia and America and probably in England too, although I'm not familiar with the current state of play in that country. There are also young men in similar situations who have been, and are being, as exploited and abused as I was, and the closeness of some of the new women's networks has exacerbated their situation. I know many of them personally and grieve for them. It makes me think that being a woman might have been a relatively minor problem in the mending of my broken career. The real blame probably lies in lack of funding and in the inertia and unwillingness of administrators at all levels to work for real equality of opportunity across the gender lines. We all long to be praised, valued, and appropriately rewarded no matter what sex we are.

Because there was an understandable but erroneous assumption that I'd been promoted on the grounds that I was a woman, some of my male colleagues at that time indulged in behavior that can only be described as squalid. In quick succession these remarks were made directly to me:

"I wish I wore a skirt."

"Of course you don't deserve it."

"I knew you'd get it. It was the year of the women."

"I'll apply when I've had a sex change."

"Who did you sleep with?"

If these things were being said to my face, I couldn't imagine what was being said behind my back. I was stunned and desperately hurt, having worked with these people for over a decade. In other circumstances and at other times they were my dear friends. Their bitter, personally directed anger was, I chose to believe, part of an overall anger against a promotion system so apparently shocking as to value teaching together with, but *above*, publications, qualifications, research, committee work, reputation, "networking," and mateship.

"Mateship" made me incredibly angry. "Mates" who were "good blokes" had been passed over, so of course the males on the staff were upset. Until my promotion I had held "mateship" in high regard as a positive and peculiarly Australian phenomenon, best illustrated in hard times like war, drought, and the depression. After my promotion I regarded it with venom as a menace perpetuated by men whose unswerving yet laudable support for each other made them blind to the needs, hardships, talents, and feelings of women.

The reaction to my advancement was partly my own fault; in the staff room to this day I play the fool and act the clown. I don't ask to be taken seriously in public. In 1986 my colleagues knew about *Possum Magic*, of course, but my children's writing was of minor relevance to my promotion, although I'm sure that many of them thought otherwise. In those dark days after my promotion only a few knew that I'd had papers published in international journals, not many knew of my academic standing in Australia, and even fewer realized that I was in demand as a speaker in the U.S.A. I was just "Mem." Three or four men were genuinely pleased at my success and said so, but they were the exceptions.

I will never forget, nor will I be allowed to forget since the sexist comments still slide around the staff room when no one's quite listening, that many of my male colleagues believed my promotion to be preposterous. However, once I'd calmed down and could view the situation more rationally, I forgave my detractors because I was fond of them after all and I realized that they couldn't help having been born male. Neither had they chosen their stereotypic attitudes. Conditioning has made us all prisoners of our sex. And even as I forgave them I raged at the female conditioning that encouraged me to make excuses for the inexcusable behavior of men.

10

Cancer

In late November 1977 I decided to have a mole removed
from my left shoulder. Anti-Cancer Foundation pamphlets
had been scattered all over the staff lounge at the college
and I had read one. Moles were mentioned. I'm covered with
moles so I read that section with extra care. Yes, I had one
mole that seemed to be growing. Yes, it was getting blacker.
Yes, I'd had a lifetime of sun. I wasn't worried. I decided to
have it removed as a precaution because I wanted to get
tanned in the summer and thought it sensible not to tempt
fate. I went off to the doctor, without telling the family,
quite jauntily on a Friday afternoon. The operation was

minor, under local anesthetic. I was so confident that I thought it was funny when the doctor asked for a sharper needle. I could tell he was having trouble stitching with the blunt one. He asked me to come back in a week. I felt great.

On Tuesday evening the phone rang while we were having dinner. Malcolm pulled the phone onto the table and took the call. I couldn't tell who was on the other end, but Malcolm's face told me that he was hearing bad news and I felt sorry for him. I would comfort him when he'd hung up. He put back the phone and said, "That was the doctor. It's serious. Your mole's come back from pathology, and he's booked you into the specialist at twelve tomorrow morning." So! My mole was malignant. Suddenly, I had real cancer. Like most people, I'd thought skin cancer was no problem. My parents-in-law and six-year-old Chloë were sitting at the table. I couldn't ask questions. I hadn't finished eating. There was trifle in the bowl and I like trifle, but I got up and threw it in the bin. I felt as if I were falling through space and would fall forever. I didn't want anyone to see my face.

I can't remember much of that evening. In between my spinning thoughts, I think I watched television. I didn't cry when I sang Chloë her nighttime song. Malcolm went out to a school-play dress rehearsal. He had to: he was the director. When he came home we sat in our big black chair together and talked around the subject, not about it. We were too scared to say what was on our minds. We were shy, like strangers.

Always in the past the great strength of our marriage had been the endless open chattiness of it. We'd talk for hours in the evening, discussing politics, work, home, us, money, travel, Chloë. We'd argue about the demarcation of jobs

106

around the house and I always proved that I did more than he did, but he used to think the argument could go no further once he'd said, "But who goes onto the roof in a storm to clean out the gutters?" We used to howl with laughter when we were on our own. Now, suddenly, we couldn't talk at all, just when we needed to most.

I could understand why. Together we were strong, but if I'd gone to pieces he would have broken down too. I wish he had. The tension was terrible. I was aching to cry my eyes out while he hugged me and told me it would be all right. But I knew him well enough to understand why he didn't want to cry. So I didn't cry either.

Later, unbeknown to me, he did cry. We had a close friend, Graham, who was a doctor. After my operation he told me that Malcolm had been up to see him that night when we couldn't talk, and that he had sat in Graham's car and cried for half an hour. Malcolm only told me that he had been to Graham's and that Graham had said that 25 percent of people with malignant melanoma died. I heard the words, but they had no meaning. Having cancer was so amazing that I actually felt important, and I knew that I would be very important to the people who loved me. It made me feel great, somehow. I fell asleep quickly that night and slept well.

The specialist was efficient and friendly. I told him that I was an intelligent professional woman and that I wanted to cope with all the information available. He wasn't impressed. He showed me the pathology report and explained that my mole was already in the second stage of cancer. By the third and fourth stages, when it has spread too far to be cut out, there is no hope. I asked him a thousand eager, anxious questions. Will I live? When will I die? What is my future? What happens next? He refused to say I would not die within five years. He conceded that if I survived for five years I would probably live a normal life span. He made me promise never to sunbathe again. "Pale is beautiful from now on, Mrs. Fox." He advised me not to have any more children because pregnancy might create the hormonal changes that trigger off growth in lurking cancer cells. I was excited and asked for that in writing because by then I was tired of people asking when I was going to have my second child. It seemed like a great excuse. He told me to check into the hospital at nine the following morning.

That same night I went to see Malcolm's production of *Julius Caesar* and had coffee and cupcakes with the School Council afterwards. I behaved graciously, astounded all the time that I had cancer and could stand there talking about macramé to the deputy head.

The next morning, before Chloë went to school, I hugged her till her bones nearly broke and hid my face in her hair to stop myself from crying. She knew I was going to hospital, but nothing had shaken her belief in my immortality. She wasn't scared and neither was I, at that point. Not really.

The operation resulted in a great chunk being removed from the top of my back. I had to lie on my stomach for twenty-four hours afterwards so that nothing touched the skin grafting onto the wound. They had sliced pieces of skin off my thigh to use for the graft. The shoulder was fine, but the thigh was excruciating. I didn't realize how bad the shoulder wound was until I saw a student nurse look at it and flinch. Malcolm went pale when he saw it although he had been warned it would be rather ghastly. This made me curious, so as soon as I was allowed to move I sneaked into the bathroom by myself. It was a raw, bloody hole as big and as deep as a teacup. It was truth staring me in the face, bawling out, "Poor thing, you're going to die!"

That night I howled with my whole body. A nurse stayed with me and allowed her fingers to be crushed and recrushed by mine. I didn't want nurses. I wanted my mother. I cried miserably in the smallest child part of me. It was Mum I needed, desperately. But my mother was countries away and didn't even know what had happened. I cried in anger, too, at the shocking idea that anybody should expect me to die at thirty-one. It was incredible. I cried for Malcolm, who would cry over our photo albums when I had died. I cried because he couldn't cook and I cried because I couldn't think of anyone for him to marry. And then I cried because I could.

When I thought of Chloë I sobbed until I thought the sadness would numb me. Die? Me! I'd raved over her kindergarten paintings like Picasso's mother. I'd taken her to the Eiffel Tower in Paris because of the Madeline books. I'd hidden soppy notes in her school lunchbox. Who else would do all that? Their loss of me was much more catastrophic than my loss of life. I couldn't bear to think of it and tried to sob myself into oblivion.

If I had died, Chloë would have been motherless, Malcolm might never have been truly happy again, and *Possum Magic* would never have been written. Having cancer once means that whenever I feel absolutely exhausted, or find an imaginary lump on my neck, or have a mouth ulcer for longer than a week, I'm certain it's cancer once more and I am dizzy with fear. Blood rushes to my face, and my knees long to give way. It's silly now to be so terrified, because I'm all right, but one of the major reasons for writing this autobiography when only half my life is over is because I'm aware that half a life may be all that I'm allowed. Cancer is still often on my mind.

I was in hospital for less than a week. By the time I came out I had rehearsed in my head the tape I was going to make for Chloë's twenty-first birthday. I had also worked out the sequence of my step-by-step cookery book for Malcolm with household hints at the end of it like "How to use Ajax and a toothbrush around the bottoms of the bath taps." That was over fourteen years ago. The hole in my shoulder has filled in, although a hideous scar remains. I haven't made the tape. The recipe book is still unwritten. I'm still here in 1991 and it looks as if I'll live as long as my grandfather did. He died at ninety-six.

11

Telling Tales

I became a storyteller because W.B. Yeats wanted me to be one although he didn't exactly rise from the grave, point a finger at me, and croak through an Irish mist, "Mem Fox, storytelling needs you!" It was a little less direct than that. Yeats and his fellow poet John Masefield were passionate about the art of storytelling and feared that without concerted action it would die out, so when Rose Bruford, who was a friend of theirs, set up her drama school, they asked her to include a course on storytelling, which she did. I loved it, probably because my mother had given me years of compulsory practice in church. The idea was to tell the story without the book, not to read it. We used literary language, certainly, but on no account were we allowed to learn our stories by heart, word for word. We had to "talk" them, much like friends exchanging gossip. Rote learning, we soon discovered, created the stiff tone of a recitation, thereby ruining the relaxed and chatty style essential for storytelling in its truest form.

After drama school, lack of practice and purpose made me forget that I was a storyteller. I put my skills in the bottom drawer of my mind and might never have used them again except that I was asked to be involved in a storytelling workshop.

In 1976, the South Australian School Libraries Branch, inspired by a group of storytellers from Victoria, decided to run a storytelling seminar for teachers and librarians. A friend of mine who was too busy to take part suggested that I replace her. Eight years had passed since my storytelling days and I'd forgotten one didn't *read.* I turned up at the planning meeting with books in my briefcase but realized, as I listened, that it was *telling* that was under discussion. I felt suddenly inadequate. Would I still be able to do it?

I learned by heart a section from the Ian Serraillier version of *Beowulf*—it was a poem so the "by heart" bit was all right. Then I learned, but not by heart, the story of Dick Whittington, and the story of Samson and Delilah from the Bible, but in modern language, from David Kossof's book of Bible stories.

All at once I was a storyteller. I found myself traveling the length and breadth of Australia telling stories in schools, hospitals, libraries, shopping centers, and parks, at conferences and seminars. During my teaching breaks I visited

112

outback settlements in the far north of Western Australia, isolated communities in South Australia, tiny schools in Tasmania, Catholic schools in Melbourne, rural schools in New South Wales, disadvantaged schools in Queensland, and aboriginal schools in the Northern Territory. Off the beaten track I went, a grateful tourist at work, at the request and at the expense of education departments around the country. I often wonder if the surprising sales of *Possum Magic* are due in part to the fact that I was a moderately well-known storyteller for many years before I became a published writer.

I had a repertoire of about twenty-five stories then. I think I can still tell fifteen of them at the drop of a hat. They are not my own. They come from folk traditions, the brothers Grimm, Hans Christian Andersen, the Bible, picture books, Jewish storybooks, and so on. My favorite age group as an audience for storytelling are the fifteen-year-olds in Year Nine because their teachers are always so thrilled to see them silent, absorbed, and perfectly behaved for an entire and unbelievable hour. Such are the spells that stories weave. Sadly, my writing life is now too time consuming to permit much storytelling. The only people to whom I still regularly tell stories are my own students (and Malcolm and Chloë).

In 1982, Margot Phillipson from the ABC heard me telling stories at a conference and decided that storytelling would be marvelous for television. She approached me about it.

"Margot," I said, "storytelling on TV? Heavens, no! Where's the audience reaction so essential for any storyteller? Where's the intimacy? Who'll listen to talking heads on television? There's no movement, no acting, you know. You just tell."

"I know," said Margot. "I've seen you do it."

For a year I resisted. It seemed wrong, somehow. Story-telling was a noble, ancient art. Television was modern technology. How could the two coexist? I was battered down in the end into believing it would work. Two series were produced between 1983 and 1986 and shown twice a year for several years on ABC TV education programs. "Once upon a time . . ." proved to be an irresistible lure, even on television.

Memorable experiences occurred in the filming of the programs, such as falling off a tomb backwards with my legs flailing the air, which reduced the camera crew to tears of laughter when they should have been crying sad tears for the soldier in the story.

The most unforgettable experience happened during the filming of a moving Hans Christian Andersen story called "The Little Matchgirl." It began with snow falling. One of the crew stood on the top of a high ladder and slowly emptied "snow"—a bag of polystyrene bits like the stuff in beanbags—onto the set. In I walked. As I breathed in before the second line, I spluttered on a piece of polystyrene, and choked and laughed and crudely spat. Each story was one "take"—the whole thing had to be perfect from the first word to the last, with no breaks. We had to start again.

Back we went to our starting positions. I watched the floor manager's arm with my heart pounding. When her arm went down I had to enter. One of the stage managers began pumping in the dry ice to make the fog. He pumped such a *thick* fog that I couldn't see the floor manager although she was waving like a windmill. We collapsed again.

During the third take everything went well until the little

matchgirl lit her first match. I struck a long match against a wall to which some matchbox stuff had been applied. Whoosh. It blazed. The story said, " . . . but the match went out, leaving nothing but a burnt-out stub in her hand," so I shook the match until it went out and laid the burnt-out stub in my tattered apron. Except that it was still alight. I felt its warmth. I continued with the story, hoping distractedly that it would eventually go out. The match got warmer. And warmer. "Oh Granny!" I said. "Please take me with you. . . . FLAMING HELL! I'M ON FIRE!!!" Leaping to my feet, I danced around the studio, flapping at my apron, shrieking. By then we were so out of control and beyond being serious that a coffee break was called before we dared to start again.

The stories I told, apart from *Koala Lou* and the Adelaide Symphony Orchestra's version of *Possum Magic*, were other people's. I didn't have the words in front of me, as some people thought. They were only in my head. It wasn't easy, and I'd hate to have to spend the rest of my life telling stories on television. I love telling stories. I love being on television. But the two together? No thanks.

The most difficult thing about telling stories on television was having to be perfect every time. In live storytelling it's fine to say, "Hey, I forgot to tell you that the princess had died by this time. Anyway the prince . . ." But on TV I couldn't do that. Another difficulty was having to say the same words each time. Like any real storyteller I changed the story slightly each time I told it. The cameramen used to fume because my words didn't fit their cues. And the other problem was workload. There were hours and hours involved in choosing the stories, learning them, and rehearsing them and then doing the takes for eight hours on a Sunday, as well as coping with everything else in my life like full-time mothering, full-time writing, and full-time teaching.

My storytelling story doesn't quite end there. In 1982 a group of South Australian storytellers met to set up the South Australian Storytelling Guild. Similar guilds had already been established in Western Australia, New South Wales, Victoria, and Tasmania. The meeting happened to be at my house on a cold, wet winter's evening. My brain must have been numb because the upshot of that little gathering was that I allowed myself to be elected inaugural president. I had never been on a committee before, let alone the president of an organization. I'm not a committee person in any way. I barely know how to propose a motion. The guild thrived, however, and still provides me with luxurious evenings lying around on cushions in other people's houses listening to stories told by different storytellers, just as our grandparents used to listen, and all the ancestors before them, since time began. It pleases me greatly to have made a contribution to this beautiful, almost lost art form.

12

Further Education, and Even Further

By 1975 I was beginning to feel uncomfortable about not having a university degree although the college seemed more than happy with my courses and my teaching. The Rose Bruford teaching diploma had stood me in excellent stead as a drama lecturer, but it hadn't proved that I am intelligent. In England the most important measure of a teacher's worth is his or her performance on the job, whereas in Australia, like America, paper qualifications have to flutter like flags in people's careers.

So I enrolled at Flinders University. Lacking in confidence, eager to please, prepared to overachieve, and aching for distinctions, I trod the familiar mature-age-student path. Chloë had just turned four and I was working full-time at Sturt.

It may seem unrelated, but three doors down the corridor from my office is the office of Mr. Hosking, who appears as one of the elderly characters in my book *Wilfrid Gordon McDonald Partridge*. The real Rick Hosking is not elderly, in fact he's younger than I am, but I used his name to honor him as a friend and because the *sk* in his name provided the alliterative quality I needed for the sentence "He listened to Mr. Hosking who told him scary stories." In 1975 Rick was a lecturer in English at Sturt C.A.E. and a tutor in English at Flinders University, whose campus was a mere three minutes away from ours.

Rick was my tutor in English. What a mortification it was to have a colleague teaching me and marking my essays! What if I were thick and he discovered it and let it slip? When I plucked up the courage to show him an early draft of my first essay, on Conrad's *Heart of Darkness*, he pointed out with tact that it might be wise to move the conclusion from the opening paragraph to the final paragraph, since conclusions normally conclude. I panicked.

Fear and frantic work were rewarded, but I thought my distinction might be a flash in the pan, since we of the mature-age-student breed take years to believe in our own capabilities in spite of the regular evidence and reassurance of high marks. I observe clones of myself in my own classes at Sturt: needlessly anxious women, desperate for approbation and success, often close to tears over assignments or the conflicting demands of homes and families, and I teach them with tenderness.

118

I hadn't expected my university education to be as lively as it turned out to be. I remember Professor Le Mire's course on Jane Austen, for instance, in which I literally groaned with pleasure over his analysis of a perfectly balanced paragraph in *Pride and Prejudice*; and John Harwood's heady extempore lectures on modern poetry, in which he impressed me with his inspired guesses as to T.S. Eliot's meanings; and Brian Matthews's riveting course on Australian literature, which revealed that such a thing as Oz Lit. exists and is more than worthy of study, Henry Lawson in particular. I remember excitement. I was always excited about language and the way writers used it.

In 1975, the year I started at Flinders, Chloë left kindergarten and started school at Cabra, aged almost four and a half, togged up in a winter uniform, tie, blazer, the lot. Malcolm was by then teaching full-time French, Italian, and drama at Cabra and he would visit her at lunchtime, concerned about her long day in the new discipline of school. But she, being an only child and gregarious, loved school and would wave a half-eaten chicken leg at him, unconcerned.

As is the case with so many other working mothers, child minding was a bother. It had been one reason for sending Chloë to school early. For two and a half days a week from the age of three, she'd been cared for by a dear friend whose daughter was roughly the same age as ours and needed companionship. Malcolm and I looked after Chloë the rest of the time. At first when I left her she'd cry, and I'd cry buckets as I drove to work, unable to see that there were probably other mothers along the way also crying their eyes out for the same reason. A quick phone call would reveal her

119

squealing with happiness over some game or other, but I never escaped the guilty feeling that I might be failing as a mother by having a job I loved and wouldn't give up.

Another reason for sending her to school was that she seemed ready for it and proved it by learning to read within two weeks although she wasn't quite four and a half. Amazed, I went to the school to shower my grateful congratulations on her teacher.

"She can read *The Foot Book* by Dr. Seuss," I announced with disbelief. "How did you do it?"

The teacher smiled and said, "I didn't. You did."

I hadn't known then what I know now about the importance of reading aloud to children, but I'd done it anyway, not for educational reasons but because of the pure pleasure of interacting with my little kid as we read piles of wonderful books together.

I think Chloë was more aware of my studying, because of the amount of time it took, than she was of my teaching. To her, teaching happened in the daytime, and my studying happened at night. Like all the other mature-age-student mothers around the country I used to have to drag myself from my child's bedside to write essays, read set books, and prepare tutorial papers, on top of all my usual work. One evening, when Chloë was six, I remember saying, "I have to go, my darling. I've got to start my Jane Austen essay."

"Oh, no!" she moaned. "I hope it's not going to be as bad as *Paradise Lost.*"

She would often, by chance, develop croup just when I was at my most fraught, trying to finish a major essay. As I knelt at her bed, sleepless with maternal anxiety, listening to her raspy breaths and watching the water from her vaporizer dripping down the walls, I'd wonder if it were some kind of divine punishment for not being a "normal" mother.

In 1978, the final year of my B.A., I began simultaneously my B.Ed. at Sturt. In spite of the fact that I was teaching more than a full load, I'd decided that as an educator I needed urgently to catch up on all the theory I'd deliberately missed at drama school. Being taught by my colleagues no longer threatened me. Doubling up on courses for one year meant I was able to complete both the B.A. and the B.Ed. by November 1979, by which time I felt like a redrafted essay myself, all cut and pasted and tattered. I was exhausted and determined never to study again.

Only a couple of years later, however, storytelling beckoned me into a new study trap. The once-upon-a-time aspect of my life had resulted in invitations to run storytelling workshops at a variety of conferences, one of which was the Australian Reading Association's annual conference in Perth in 1979. Although I was a drama lecturer who knew nothing about the teaching of reading, I attended all the plenary sessions out of interest and was all shook up, as Elvis Presley might have said, to hear of great shifts in the theory and practice of the teaching of reading, writing, listening, and speaking, which I now know as "language arts." The experience was akin to a religious conversion. Certainly it changed my life.

Because the college urgently needed another staff member with expertise in the teaching of reading and writing, the opportunity to retrain fell into my supplicating hands in 1981, and I was given a year's leave on full pay to do it.

The dull syllables of "a Graduate Diploma in Language Arts from the Underdale Campus of the South Australian

C.A.E." bear no relation to the fireworks of my learning in that institution. Guided by teachers like Adeline Black, Barbara Comber, and Mike Dilena, I was introduced to a sparkling world of knowledge in which some of my old beliefs were exploded as new ideas were presented. My brain blazed into top gear as it explored issues such as how children learn language, how we read, why we read, how to teach reading more effectively, defining the writing process, teaching writing, teaching literature, and developing productive talking and listening in classrooms. The articles I read and the papers I wrote challenged my own practice as a teacher of anything, not merely as a teacher of the English language. The art of teaching became and remains a vital and consuming interest, which is a nice irony, considering teaching was once the last thing I wanted to do.

In that year, 1981, I spent an enlightening week at a residential writing workshop run by Barbara Kamler at the then–Riverina C.A.E. in New South Wales. In the mornings and evenings we wrote; in the afternoons we studied the teaching of writing at all levels. My confidence as a writer was such that I imagined I'd have little to learn, but I was shaken to discover that "room for improvement" applied also to me.

Barbara taught me to find flaws in my writing that I'd never been able to see before: small things, but important, such as an overuse of adjectives and adverbs, brackets, exclamation marks, and the word *very*; and major things such as understanding the nature of "voice" as well as the difference between "telling": "It was hot"; and "showing," painting a picture of the quality of hotness: "I put on my sunglasses to avoid the glare, but little lakes of sweat soon formed on

the lower rims and overflowed, oozing along my cheekbones."
Understanding is different from being able to put something
into practice, of course. All at once writing became terribly
difficult.

My rapturous studies of 1981 led me inevitably along the
road to an external M.Ed. from the University of Wollon-
gong in 1986. But a fool and her study are soon parted. It
was idiotic to attempt the four careers of student, lecturer,
writer, and home-woman simultaneously. I completed two
semesters successfully and then withdrew, in a hysteria of
exhaustion, puzzled that I couldn't cope with every strand
of my frantic existence.

I tried to believe that my reputation as a writer was more
important than a higher degree and would forever be more
noticeable than a few more letters after my name, but family
influence and prevailing academic attitudes made me doubt
it. Brian Cambourne, my supervisor at the university, lifted
my spirits immeasurably in February 1988 after I'd had an
article published in the highly regarded U.S. journal *Language Arts*. He sent me a photocopy of the table of contents
with a note attached:

Dear Mem,
    *The University of Wollongong is proud of you, even if
you are no longer enrolled.*
                    Cheers,
                    Brian

Although I have no time for formal study, I do have time
to reflect on the fascinating duality of my life as a writer who
teaches writing. Whenever I'm intrigued by a new insight I

encourage myself to work it into a paper for publication or presentation at a conference so that those who read it or listen to it will be stunned into thinking that I'm actually Dr. Fox and that I choose not to use the title out of modesty. In reality an M.A. or a Ph.D. in my life is about as likely as the queen coming to tea. My studies are over. Perhaps.

13

The Writing Group

In 1981, during my retraining as a lecturer in writing and reading and related language arts, five friends and I set up a writing group that rapidly assumed importance as "The Writing Group" to those who were aware of its existence. We were all teachers of writing one way or another and had decided that we had to *be* writers if we were to *teach* writing, since this was and still is a philosophical cornerstone of our work: Those who can't do, can't teach, to parody Shaw's maxim.

Now it so happened that the group was made up entirely

of women. This was accidental. We'd been on the verge of inviting two men, but not because they were men. I can't remember why they didn't join us, but I'm glad they didn't. When the writing group started we were all married, all teachers, all mothers, and all under forty, so the common ground was vast.

We met for four months, once a week, and then less regularly for over three years, to read something— anything—we'd written for the group. Occasionally we read articles-in-progress or children's stories, for which we'd request specific responses. (This was two years before the publication of *Possum Magic*.) But our pieces were more often musings and reflections on what it was like to be us.

We met on Monday evenings, usually at the house of Joelie Hancock, around whose ample kitchen table we'd sit in extraordinary fellowship for over four hours. Adeline, late, and full of excuses, smoking fit to kill all night, would read us illuminating pieces about her American childhood and hilarious pieces about her children. Jennie, always immaculate, let us peep through her writing at her darkening marriage and we'd offer specious advice and lots of love. Chris, just in from an outback settlement—she was an adviser in aboriginal education at the time—would twist our hearts with the pathos of her motherhood and paint such funny, clear pictures of hotels in the bush that we hoped we'd never have to stay in them. Barb, one of whose children was always ill (surely not "always" although it seemed so) would make us laugh over her laconic stories, like the one about her very Irish wedding. Joelie would peel off her persona and parade her private thoughts, which were often so unexpected we'd sit back, dazed.

126

And me? I used to write pieces about money, since we were always short of it, always traveling it away overseas every summer, leaving too little for essentials like food and clothing and cars that worked. And I'd also write pieces called "When I'm Old . . ." that painted a rosy picture of living alone, in great wealth, with Malcolm next door for companionship whenever I needed it. The duties of a wife, housewife, and mother weighed more negatively upon me then. In between the readings we'd react to each other's pieces and eat Joelie's pâté and banana cake and drink Joelie's Riesling and then her Earl Grey.

Sometimes, when finding a topic grew difficult, we'd set a theme for the week, like "Childbirth" or "My Father." "Motherhood" came up over and over again. I can be so maudlin, and have been, about being a mother that I thought I'd better risk at least one of my writing-group pieces to correct the public and private balance of my maternal feelings. Do I love motherhood? Bah! Not always! How's this, for a motherhood statement?

It Isn't Marriage That Gets Me Down

It isn't marriage that gets me down, it's motherhood. I've been a bit depressed ever since I got back from Sydney and I wondered what it was. Of course life has been exciting—what with *Possum Magic* launches and radio interviews and signings and the excitement of friends and family and all that. But I felt I ought to be woman enough to cope with a scaling down of adrenaline-producing activity. Last night, as I was mint-tea-ing with Malk, I felt tears of depression creeping down my face at the thought of having to live with Chloë for perhaps another ten years.

She's driving me up the wall. She isn't naughty or bad—she's just Chloë. But being "just Chloë" means a great deal. She speaks loudly and she speaks all the time—mealtimes, bedtimes, walk-on-the-beach-times. All the time. She's witty so I can't ignore her and when I've laughed once she's encouraged and makes me laugh again.

At night just as she's dropping off she'll launch into a hysterical description of the pillows she encounters on school camps. I *long* to leave but she holds me with magic words that make me laugh in spite of myself. Even when she's occupied *quietly* in her room I can feel her noisy, demanding presence permeating the house.

She treats me as an inferior very often, bossing me about as if she were my mother: Don't do this. Don't do that. I hope you're not going out dressed like that! Don't get too excited over *Possum Magic*—pride comes before a fall. Talk talk talk talk. What's for tea? Oh God, well, I'm not eating *that!* Are you going to work? Who's going to give me breakfast? (With tears in her eyes.) She is perfectly capable of making a million breakfasts but it's more exciting to blackmail, to be dependent, to make her presence felt as deeply and as often as possible.

Malcolm and I should never have married. Our child is what you'd expect. And I can't bear it. I wish she'd leave me *alone!* I don't want to be a mother anymore. It's boring and exhausting.

I want to be ALONE!

We were supposed to give each other constructive criticism, but we either laughed until we cried, cried until we laughed, or wandered off on tangents that were deep and meaningful. It was such a warm time. Driving down to Joelie's each week I'd be really pleased about seeing the others again, and I could never wait to read out my writing even though it was usually a dashed-off first draft. In our learning about the nature of writing we grew to understand, above all, that writers write willingly if an audience is there and is likely to be sympathetic to the content of a piece before wading in to criticize its form.

When it transpired, early on, that there would be no males in The Writing Group I was appalled. I'd always had a pleasant, bantering interaction with men and hadn't much enjoyed my experiences of women-only groups. I was worried that a "hen-party" superficiality would develop. The reverse was true. The Writing Group revealed to me how supportive women could be towards women, how much in common we had, what a secret club women were, and how men couldn't join, no matter what. The subtle and gross differences between men's and women's value systems, their perceptions, and their friendships were explored and clarified. How relieved we were to be women! Emotionally, we decided, it would be pretty ghastly to be a man. And lonely, too.

The Writing Group meets rarely now, perhaps once a year for old times' sake. Our last meeting was to celebrate, in her West Australian absence, Jennie's second marriage. I wore my wedding veil. Chris wore her wedding dress. We drank champagne and reread some of our past pieces about love and marriage. In our reminiscences, what amazed us most was that we'd had enough time, when we were younger, to meet once a week. Now we're all so career-oriented, so busy, that there's hardly time to breathe once a week, let alone think of a topic to write about.

The Writing Group was invaluable to me as a woman, and salutary for me as a writer. I mourn its passing. When we're all retired maybe we'll meet again to write again, to read new pieces that begin "Being a grandmother . . ."

14

Possum Magic

During their final eight-week teaching practice a number of my students choose to work in isolated schools on the west coast of South Australia. In June 1989, at the invitation of their principals, I toured their schools for a week wearing my writer's hat. Authors don't often venture into such far-flung areas, so the buildup for my visit had been intense and had involved weeks of work. On my second-last day, at Wudinna Area School, a small boy aged about six looked at me and said seriously, "Are you really Mem Fox?"

"Yes, I am," I replied.

131

"And did you *really* write *Possum Magic?*"

"Yes, I did."

He leaned forward. "I'm *sick* of *Possum Magic!*" he said with a weary sigh.

Where did it all start? In 1978 I studied children's literature at Flinders University as part of my B.A. The lecturer, Felicity Hughes, to whom I owe so much, set as an assignment the writing of a children's story. As a typical, overachieving mature-age student, I secretly thought the assignment beneath me. I felt it was below the rigorous university standard I'd come to expect. Felicity had taught me Milton's *Paradise Lost* in a stunning course during which I'd read all twelve books and written a good essay. Children's Literature, I felt sure, would be intellectually less worthy of my attention. I'd enrolled in it only for Chloë's sake, because she was an avid reader at six, and I wanted to update my knowledge of books for children.

When I sat down and attempted to write my story I discovered how difficult it was to transfer the ideas in my head to the paper on my desk. The words wouldn't come right. The tone was nauseating, the plot too involved. I was angry. After all it was only a children's story, wasn't it? It couldn't be that difficult. I realized why Felicity had given us the assignment in the first place: so that never again would we underestimate the skills required in being able to write for children. With new understanding we continued the course, placing children's authors respectfully on a literary pedestal as we tried to become authors ourselves.

For two reasons I decided to write an overtly Australian story. First, Chloë loved reading, and I was upset to find that there weren't many recent Australian books for her age group, apart from *The Bunyip of Berkley's Creek* and *The Giant Devil Dingo*. She loved those. So did I. There was, I felt, a need for more books like them, absolutely unique to Australia, that Australian children could take to their hearts. I'd loved *Blinky Bill* and *Snugglepot and Cuddlepie* as a child. I wanted to write a book that would carry the same weight of national pride. This was before everyone, including Australians themselves, suddenly fell in love with Australia and everything in it.

I also wrote the story for Malcolm, who was returning to England every Christmas because, for him, it was "home." I wanted him to be happy and at home in Australia. So I wrote about an invisible mouse called Hush who lived in England with her grandmother. Her grandma, who could make magic, had made Hush invisible to save her from cats, but couldn't remember how to make her visible again except that it was something to do with food. So they tried fish and chips in England, snails in France, spaghetti in Italy, moussaka in Greece, and curry in India without success. Finally they came to Australia. In Adelaide a lamington made Hush's tail appear. In a schoolyard a vegemite sandwich made her legs and body appear, and in a grand hotel a pavlova made her head appear. They lived in Australia happily ever after.

Because I was a mature-age student and therefore keen for an excellent grade, I was worried that Felicity might think the story wasn't up to scratch, so I decided to try and blind her to the imperfections in my work by asking an artist to paint me a few illustrations that I could hand in with it. I asked one of my colleagues, Tom Gleghorn, an artist and an art lecturer, if he could recommend someone.

"Try Julie Vivas in Sydney," he said. "I taught her in art school. She paints in watercolor and she's brilliant."

He was right. Julie's illustrations were beyond my wildest imaginings. Her composition and technique were out of this world and I adored the sense of humor escaping from each painting. "I love this woman," I thought. We hadn't even met at this point. Nor had we talked to each other on the phone. I had promised Julie in a letter that I'd try to have the book published, but that in the meantime I couldn't pay her anything. In retrospect that was outrageous, but she didn't complain.

Felicity gave me a distinction for the assignment—hah! Perhaps the illustrations had tricked her after all—and she strongly encouraged me to send it to a publisher. Over the next five years nine publishers turned down *Hush the Invisible Mouse*. Each time I received a rejection slip I felt ashamed that I'd dared to believe it might be worth publishing. Humiliated, I'd hide it away. Once it sat at the bottom of my wardrobe for eighteen months. One publisher said the language was too flamboyant. So I changed it. Another said there were millions of mice in children's literature and it was therefore far too boring a story for her to publish. One said it was too Australian, thereby enraging me to frothing point. I kept fiddling with the story, rewriting it every time someone rejected it, and then sending it off to someone else. Another publisher said the illustrations would be too expensive to reproduce. One gave no reason at all.

Two people gave me the courage to continue because they believed in the book. One was Malcolm, who would come home exasperated after he'd been browsing in bookshops.

134

"You should see the kids' books on those shelves! Badly illustrated, badly written, the weakest plots in the world! How did they get published? Take out yours and try again."

The other was Sandra Gapper, a teacher-librarian. Because she was an expert in children's literature and loved my story, I was able to keep renewing my confidence in it. Dejected, I'd phone her with the news of each rejection, but by the time we'd finished our conversation, with her "Don't give up" ringing in my ears, I'd feel less crushed, less of an imbecile. She even made me feel I had potential.

The breakthrough came in 1982. My teachers' handbook, *How to Teach Drama to Infants Without Really Crying*, had been accepted for publication by Ashton Scholastic. (The book was published in the U.S. as *Teaching Drama to Young Children*.) I was beside myself. A colleague and I were side by side leafing through catalog cards in the college library. John Palmer was his name. My concentration floated out of the library window. I couldn't work out whether *j* came before *q*. Jumpy with excitement, I finally blurted out, "John, I've got some excellent news."

"Mmmm?"

"I've had a book accepted for publication!"

"Tell me."

I told him.

"Didn't know you wrote books," he said. "Got any more lying around? I know a new publisher. Just set up. In Adelaide. Looking for manuscripts. Called Omnibus Books."

I went, agitated, to Omnibus late one afternoon in June. It's unusual to be able to call on a publisher in Adelaide since there are so few of them. There I sat, in dead silence, picking at my yellow sweater, staring at the rush matting on

135

the floor, gazing out of the window at the bus station over the road (hence "Omnibus" Books), letting my coffee go cold, real coffee, they never drink instant at Omnibus, while my manuscript was read. It wasn't rejected. It wasn't accepted. Sue Williams, one of the publishers, doted on the illustrations. I think they said, "Don't ring us, we'll ring you," but I could be wrong. I stumbled out, hoping I hadn't humiliated myself once again.

A few days later—it was a Monday, I remember that clearly—the phone rang in my office. It was Jane Covernton, another of the publishers at Omnibus. Jane always talks slowly. She seemed, on this occasion, to pause for a lifetime between each word.

"Oh, hi, Mem. . . . It's Jane . . . from Omnibus. We think we'll do . . . *Hush.*"

The phone zinged away from my ear. Had I heard right? I'd waited five years for this moment. Yes! I had heard right. I rang Malcolm's school nearly sobbing for joy and asked the school secretary to please please get Malcolm Fox to the phone, it was diabolically urgent, it didn't matter what class he was in, please please as quickly as she could, I needed him very badly and I was sure the school wouldn't mind, please please. As soon as I'd knocked him over with my news, I leaped out of my office and jumped in circles down the corridor.

From then things moved fast. I was asked to cut the story from three and a half pages of single-spaced typing to one and a half pages of double-spaced typing. Two thirds of it chopped in one blow! Jane, in her instructions as to the rewriting, told me to go away and "be lyrical."

"And hurry up about it as well," said Sue.

They went to Sydney and Melbourne to carry out market research. Mice, it seems, were in plague proportions in children's books. The mice had to go. And why not keep the journey confined to Australia? Make it an all-Australian book? Why hadn't I thought of it myself! We debated as to which Australian animal we'd use to replace the mouse. It couldn't be a koala because of *Blinky Bill,* and kangaroos were too obvious. I have possums on my roof. Their babies are adorable. Possums it was! I made a tiny, thirty-two-page booklet, rewrote the story as lyrically as I could, and called it *Possum Magic.*

"*Possum Magic . . .* yeah, I like that," Sue grunted. She's a great grunter. We all liked it, although we sat around with our real coffee, fiddling with this page and that sentence, for weeks, saying—"How about . . . ?" and "I know! What if . . ." and "Try this . . ." How we worked! How I struggled.

The last thing to come good was the first paragraph. I spent four hours on a Sunday afternoon squeezing up pieces of paper viciously and sweeping them off the dining-room table with my arm. After twenty-two attempts, and tears of frustration, I spoke to myself severely.

"Look, just say what you mean! 'Once upon a time . . . but not very long ago (because they didn't have pavlovas and vegemite long ago) deep in the Australian bush there lived two possums. Their names were Hush and Grandma Poss.' Hey! I've got it!" And I had, as soon as I'd removed the words in brackets.

Years later I was to discover, astonished, that the pauses, the phrasing, and the when, the where, and the who in the first paragraph of *Possum Magic* mirrored exactly the opening verse of the Biblical story of Ruth, which I'd learned by heart at drama school seventeen years before:

Now it came to pass, in the days when the judges ruled, that there was a famine in the land. And a certain man of Bethlehem, Judah, went to sojourn in the country of Moab, he, and his wife, and his two sons . . .

On March 31, 1983, nine months after they'd accepted it, Sue and Jane came to my house to deliver personally the first copy of *Possum Magic*. I stroked it as if it were made of silk. This beautiful book was mine! I hugged it. I was a writer.

Possum Magic was launched in the reception room of the Sydney Opera House in May. The first edition of five thousand had already sold out. Julie and I met each other at last, and she didn't hold against me the fact that the change to possums had made it necessary to paint all the illustrations again. Two of the original mouse illustrations now grace my walls.

I'd decided it would be wonderful to be able to tell my grandchildren truthfully that I had "sung at the great Sydney Opera House, my darlings." I could see their eyes widen. So, shaking out my drama training in this bright new spotlight, I sang a thank-you song to the tune of "Early One Morning," instead of making a speech. Sue-from-Omnibus said, "What did you want to do that for?"

The South Australian launch of *Possum Magic* was a more homely, grotty affair in the student bar at Sturt College. I asked everyone I knew and forced them all to eat vegemite sandwiches. Graeme Speedy, my charismatic boss, launched the book. Neither he nor I nor anyone else could have guessed the amazing future that awaited *Possum Magic*. It was a children's book, and that was all.

I must have read *Possum Magic* to children and adults over a thousand times, but I never tire of it. I love its words. I love its rhythms. I love its feelings. I love its pictures. I love its Australianness. And I'm still excited and as thrilled as can be over its unexpected success. It's become the best-selling children's book in Australia's history: over four hundred thousand copies sold in seven years, in Australia alone. A phenomenon, rather than a book. A normal print run is between five thousand and ten thousand. For me, it has gone beyond being a book. It lives and breathes, and Grandma Poss has taken on the status of a best friend. Whenever I see a dead possum on the road I catch my breath in sorrow, hoping it isn't her.

In the year after their publication, children's books in Australia are eligible for the Children's Book Council awards. In 1984, librarians, teachers, parents, children, and booksellers all told me that there'd never been such an open-and-shut case as to the winner of the Picture Book of the Year. *Possum Magic* would win, without doubt. It was, according to them, a foregone conclusion. But they hadn't read the strict rules by which the judges are required to operate, nor had any of them been judges themselves.

Nevertheless, I chose to believe them. My two front teeth had long been stained from old fillings and looked awful, so I had them capped before the awards in case my photo appeared in the *Advertiser*. I also bought the most expensive dress I have ever owned.

On the Friday night of the ceremony, which happened

to be in my home state that year, I walked into the Festival Centre behind a woman wearing a dress exactly the same as mine. And *Possum Magic* didn't win. It came second, with "highly commended." And Pamela Allen, who won with *Bertie and the Bear*, wasn't able to be there to receive the award. For me, at least, it was an appalling evening.

Next morning I opened the magazine section of the *Advertiser* to be confronted by a huge photo of a girl and a boy and a dog reading *Possum Magic*. The critic must also have expected *Possum Magic* to win. After I'd read the lovely things she'd written I crawled back into bed and sobbed into Malcolm's shoulder. I minded very much that it had not won. I will always mind.

Later in 1984, *Possum Magic* won the medal for the Best Children's Book of the Year in the N.S.W. Premier's Literary Awards. I flew to Sydney for the occasion. Julie Vivas and I were like ignorant country bumpkins as we sat at a table with famous people in the writing world, none of whom we recognized, in the flashy atmosphere of the Sydney Opera House. It was only later that we discovered who they all were: publishers, poets, agents, editors, Australia Council luminaries, and so on. I was impressed by the fact that Les Murray of the potbelly and poetry prize that year accepted his award dressed in jeans and a blue singlet. I had worn my expensive *Possum Magic* dress.

In my speech (which I did not sing on this occasion) I told the story of how I'd wasted my time having my teeth capped earlier in the year and what a disappointment the Children's Book Council awards had been, considering the book's undoubted success. With mock emotion I said, "I'm deeply grateful to you, Mr. Wran. Not only have you made my teeth worthwhile, your prize will help me pay my dentist's bill." As I stepped down from the microphone, the eminent historian Manning Clark tapped me on the arm and whispered, "My teeth aren't all my own either." And Thomas Keneally said he thought my speech had been very witty. Perhaps he'd had a drink or two.

In the same year *Possum Magic* was performed on ABC educational television as the finale of the "Storytelling with Mem Fox" series. Music had been specially composed by Mike Kenny of the ABC and had been played by the Adelaide Symphony Orchestra in the television studios. The fact that I couldn't read music or beat time correctly hadn't been a disaster. Somehow I'd coped, even if the orchestra had suffered constant alarms throughout every rehearsal and performance.

In 1986, a request was made to perform this version of *Possum Magic* as the finale in an ABC Family Concert in the Adelaide Festival Theatre. Live! With everyone watching me go wrong. I agreed, but I was perturbed. I can sing and I can just tell if one note of music in a score goes up or down, but I had to be able to perform a variety of musical tricks: speaking in time with the music, speaking over the music, speaking in between the music to an exact beat, and doing it all by ear and by watching the conductor. I should have said no. But I was in love with the music and couldn't bear anyone else to speak the words, so I said I'd give it a go.

Chloë, who is always anxious that I will show her up by being a big flop one way or another, came into my dressing room on the night of the performance agog with news, and relieved beyond belief. "Ma! There are women and children in the foyer crying because they can't get in. You've sold out!" I did make a few mistakes during the performance, but the atmosphere was so heartwarming and tolerant that few people noticed. I hope.

A sweet surprise occurred in mid-1987. New South Wales had set up its own award for children's books, judged by children. It was called KOALA: Kids' Own Australian Literary Award. *Possum Magic* won the junior section and was also placed highly in the senior section, which was an extra compliment. The ceremony took place at Taronga Park Zoo on a hot, hot day. The children's faces were bright red, their eyes glazed with heat. I willed them not to faint with sunstroke. They obeyed.

The following day Julie Vivas and I flew to Cowra to speak to a thousand children from nearby country schools at a *Possum Magic* picnic on Cowra Oval. It was again fearfully hot. Each child had a surprise lunch packed by the various school canteens: a vegemite sandwich, a piece of pavlova, and half a lamington. The food was warm and squishy. Julie and I stood on the back of a truck to speak to the gathered masses, who had no idea what their surprise lunches would be. As they unwrapped them they moaned, "Oh, no! I hate vegemite sandwiches!" "Mine are hot!" "Oooh, yuk, pavlova. I don't want mine. D'you wannit?"

Julie turned to me and said, "Isn't it bizarre? It's all because of our little book."

We found it difficult to conceive that we had created *Possum Magic*. It seemed not to belong to us anymore. The world had claimed it as its own. "Bizarre" was right.

The only unhappiness associated with *Possum Magic* was

a temporary misunderstanding with Julie Vivas and Omnibus over the *Possum Magic* products. At first when the birthday book, the baby book, the *Grandma Poss Cookbook*, and other similar products were launched on to the market I received nothing financially. Omnibus, whose integrity was never in question, honestly believed I had no right to profit from the artwork. I didn't think I had any right either since I was the writer, not the artist. Nor did I mind. After all, I didn't need the money. I already had a full-time job as well as a best-selling book. Nevertheless, I was persuaded by people who knew about these matters to take some action. Julie, Omnibus, and I had a marvelous relationship and I didn't want to spoil it, but something had to be done. There was anger and shouting. There were tears and lawyers. There were literary agents and fights. I wished at times that I'd never written *Possum Magic*. Julie told me later that she'd often felt the same. We all came through it, however, and made new arrangements and promises. The rocked boat was restored to its even keel, its crew settled down, and we all sailed on into calmer waters.

For me, living with *Possum Magic* happily ever after has been delayed a little by the problem of provisional tax. Being a teacher, I'd never heard of it until I had to pay it. After years of panic and hysterics around March 31, when it has to be paid, I've come to realize that half my royalties have to be saved and paid back to the government. I'm not unduly fussed by it so long as the taxes from *Possum Magic* are helping to build hospitals, or pay teachers, or provide child care rather than assisting in the export of uranium or the acquisition of defense weaponry. After tax, the ripple effect of this little book has helped a publishing house to flourish, a writer to extend her house, and an illustrator to buy a house, with all the attendant employment that those activities imply. As a ten-pound migrant I like to think I've earned my assisted passage.

15

I Think I'll Write
a Picture Book
One Day . . .

Omnibus Books, the Australian publishers of *Possum Magic*, receive around a hundred picture-book texts a week and often reject them all, including many of mine. There are subtleties in writing for children that I'll attempt to illuminate in terms of my own initial ignorance.

Like many would-be writers I made the mistake of thinking that a picture book, being short, is the easiest kind of book to write. It isn't. During the writing of every book, as I stare at the mess of crossings-out on the pages in front of me, I lean on one elbow and groan, "This is the last time I'm going through this. The very last time." I seem to remember saying something similar during childbirth. Writing and childbirth have much in common.

In the first place, I didn't know that there was a difference between an illustrated story and a picture book. The three and a half single-spaced, typed pages of *Hush the Invisible Mouse*, which I submitted unsuccessfully to nine publishers over five years, were much too long although I didn't realize it at the time. Sue and Jane at Omnibus Books kindly and belatedly pointed out that a standard picture book is always a thirty-two-page book because of the way the paper folds in the printing process into two, four, eight, sixteen, and thirty-two sections. With very few words, the illustrations reveal much of the action, character, setting, and tone.

The number of words per page has to be limited to the amount of time it takes for a child to absorb the pictures before the page is turned. Picture books are for little kids who are soon bored by long-winded narrative, but just as soon enchanted by a short and expertly illustrated text. *Possum Magic* has 512 words. *Wilfrid* has a shocking 640. *Hattie and the Fox* was my first really-truly definitive picture book because the few words depend upon the pictures—gorgeous collage illustrations by Patricia Mullins—which in turn depend upon the words. *Night Noises* and *Guess What?* are also definitive picture books.

In contrast, an illustrated story has a comparatively huge number of words on the page, illuminated by a few pictures here and there. I believe that like me, most people who want to write a picture book make the early mistake of writing a story-for-illustration instead.

I've found that it's easy but not wise to fall into the trap of thinking small-equals-brain-damaged when it comes to writing for children. They detest being patronized by a sort of "great-aunt style." Writing down to them is gloriously unsuccessful, as I demonstrated myself in *Hush the Invisible Mouse*, much of which was preachy and patronizing. Even the first couple of lines were a disaster:

Once there was a mouse. Well, was that special? This one was.

One of the elements that make the difference between forgettable and unforgettable is the quality of the writing in picture books. If the sentences have no special rhythm or structure, if the words are carelessly chosen and sloppily placed, the writing won't satisfy the reader's psyche, nor will it encourage the reader to return for another visit, and another. Fiddling with a single sentence for the best part of a day shouldn't matter: picture books are so short that it's essential the best words are placed in the best possible order.

In choosing those words my attitude is that children can understand, in the context of a good story, much more than most people give them credit for, so if I like a word I use it no matter how "difficult" it is. Children who are learning to read are perfectly capable of identifying the long words in *Possum Magic* such as *invisible, lamington,* and *vegemite,* because they're important words in the story. They're much easier to recognize than the cat-sat-on-the-mat vocabulary found in old-fashioned school readers.

I don't balk at using simile and metaphor either, since they're such useful ways to paint pictures. For example in *Night Noises* I wanted to show the age of Lily Laceby, not to tell it:

Her hair was as wispy as cobwebs in ceilings. Her bones were as creaky as floorboards at midnight.

In the same book I used metaphor to describe a storm:

Outside, clouds raced along the sky, playing hide and seek with the moon. Wind and rain rattled at the windows and trees banged against the roof.

The moment I begin to think, "Well, I'm only writing for little kids so I don't have to choose my words as carefully as Peter Carey did in *Oscar and Lucinda,*" is the moment I fail as a writer for children—and I have failed on several (published) occasions. The age of my readers should have no bearing on the level of effort I put into the writing.

The only concession I make to my young audience is in my sentence structure. It can't be too complex in case it hinders the getting across of meaning. As I write a book for children, I write it also for my adult friends, for the prime minister, and for my mother. If it isn't good enough for them, it isn't good enough for children either.

In my experience the best-loved picture books are so well written that they leave a lasting impression on the reader. My own favorites, still not displaced after so many years, are Jenny Wagner's *John Brown, Rose, and the Midnight Cat* and Anthony Browne's *Willy the Wimp.* They have a passionate quality. By *passion* I mean a constant undercurrent of tension combined with compassion, which makes readers care desperately about the fate of the main characters. It's not easy to achieve, but I'm convinced that writing without passion is writing for oblivion. *Koala Lou,* for instance, which is a story about a koala who comes second in the Bush Olympics, developed subconsciously out of my disappointment at *Possum Magic* not winning the Picture Book of the Year award, an event that hadn't been a disaster in world terms although I had bawled like a baby at the time. Coming second with "highly commended" hadn't been enough. I wanted to hide for a while, to live through my failure alone. Writing *Koala Lou* was a catharsis. The pathetic little koala out on a limb in one of the final illustrations is none other than the author herself. I'm never quite sure, when I read it aloud to an audience of any age, whether I'll be able to get through it with a steady voice. Once, in Gainesville, Florida, I cried uncontrollably in front of a large group of ten-year-olds and was so surprised by my own reaction that I laughed as well. I imagine they went home that day and said, "Mom, Mom! We had this Australian crazy in class today." I didn't mind breaking down in front of the class, because passion is to picture books as yeast is to bread: the one is nothing without the other.

I'm thrilled when other adults suddenly howl at the end of the book. It makes me dare to think it might be a "good" book, because good books have as much to do with the effect they have on the reader as with any other criterion. If we don't laugh, gasp, block our ears, sigh, vomit, giggle, curl our toes, empathize, sympathize, feel pain, weep, or shiver during the reading of a picture book, then surely the writer has wasted our time, our money, and our precious, precious trees.

Ideas for picture books seem to arise most often from real life, from the experiences of very young children: visiting Grandma, starting school, having a new baby in the house, moving to a new neighborhood, having an imaginary friend, disliking certain foods, washing the dog, the death of a pet, or even worse, of a grandparent as in my book *Sophie,* and so on. It isn't easy. My imagination is pathetically inadequate when it comes to thinking up initial ideas. I can't and never have been able to write to order. Some writers, when asked to write a story for four-year-old girls on the theme of multicultural friendships at kindergarten, can do so at the flick of a word processor. Not me, alas. One of the reasons I loathe writing picture books is because finding the idea is so difficult.

Initially *Koala Lou* came into being because in 1983 I received a letter from Pat Farrar, the friend and partner of Olivia Newton-John, Australian singer and superstar. Pat and Olivia had opened an Australian shop in America called Koala Blue (which has since opened in Australia as well), in which they were selling the newly published *Possum Magic.* They asked me to write them a story about a koala called Blue so that they could market a fluffy toy koala along with the book of the same name and make a fortune for themselves and for me. I was dead keen to make the fortune but had to send back a sad little letter explaining my inability to write to order. I promised to let them know if I had any ideas.

The Koala Blue shop was in Los Angeles. Los Angeles was to host the Olympics in 1984. An idea began to form. I always feel sorry for the Olympic competitors who come second in their events, especially some of the younger ones from Eastern Bloc countries who've spent the previous four years training in order to win. How must they feel when they go back home? What happens? Are they shunned by their friends? Do they sob in their mothers' arms? How would Koala Blue have felt if he'd come second in an Olympic event? The story began to germinate.

This is typical of my writing process. The ideas leap into my head from current events, and if they don't, I don't write and I don't mind. I'm not a disciplined writer who sits down at a blank piece of paper or a blank word-processor screen and says, "Right! I'm not moving until I've written five hundred words." That's not me at all. I could sit for a month without writing anything.

A subtheme in *Koala Lou* arose out of being the eldest of three girls. Wondering whether, or how much, my parents love me is a foolish but continuing anxiety in my life, perhaps in all our lives. Is my father pleased with the way I've turned out? Is my mother proud of me? Do they think I'm absolutely and utterly terrific, or not? In my heart of hearts I believe that they do, but I had to write *Koala Lou* just to be sure.

Getting the idea may be difficult, but actually writing it down is such torture that my shoulders ache with the tension of trying to choose the right words to put in the right places. In every book I've written, my greatest difficulties have been beginnings and endings. If things go wrong in the middle I seem to be able to accept it, but the rhythm of opening and closing lines causes me misery. Beginnings are usually too long-winded. The answer to the questions who, what, when, and where can be provided in a couple of short sentences, as in:

There was once a small boy called
Wilfrid Gordon McDonald Partridge, and what's more
he wasn't very old either. His house was

*next door to an old people's home and he
knew all the people who lived there.*

Hattie and the Fox is even more direct:

> *Hattie was a big black hen. One
> morning she looked up and said . . .*

In most of my first drafts I've taken an unnecessary page to explain what's what. I now keep the word *cut* uppermost in my mind, especially when it comes to developing the characters. I try to reveal them through what they say and do, rather than through long-winded, adjective-ridden descriptions.

Endings can be equally difficult. For almost two years the ending of *Koala Lou* went like this:

> *. . . her mother flung her arms around her neck and
> said, "Koala Lou, I DO love you. You're the best koala
> in the whole wide world!" And she hugged her for a
> very long time.*

A colleague who happened to be a psychologist wanted to know what *best* meant: "the *best* koala in the whole wide world." He didn't like it. It was inexplicit. To him it was everything bad and wrong and ugly. So I changed it to "You're the dearest koala in the whole wide world." And then I cut it out altogether because my editor circled the word *dearest* and wrote me a note in the margin of my manuscript: "Have to change this. Mother can't say this, not with other babies. You will have to think of something else. I'm sure you can do it, Mem!"

In the end the closing paragraph evolved into this:

Before she could say a word, her mother had flung
her arms around her neck and said, "Koala Lou, I DO
love you! I always have and always will." And she
hugged her for a very long time.

I couldn't have done it on my own. I had to talk it through. It's the content I need advice about, not the style. I can rewrite stylistically by reading aloud in private, but I can't tell by myself which bits of the content are missing, confusing, boring, or irrelevant.

I've learned that for me it isn't necessary to set out the manuscript as a book, although I did make a mock-up of *Guess What?* because the text was so brief and so difficult to illustrate that I had to problem-solve in a concrete fashion, page by page. Usually I present the manuscript as a short story and leave the page breaks and illustrative ideas to the publisher, who knows a great deal more than I do about the various possibilities available and doesn't take kindly to being given instructions. Hints on the content of the pictures are only appropriate when the text is literally meaningless without them.

Like many others I believed that it was up to me to find my own illustrator, and that completed illustrations had to accompany the manuscript. No! The chances of being published are halved if pictures are sent with the text. *Possum Magic* was a rare exception. The publisher finds the artist. The publisher *wants* to find the artist—it's one of the creative excitements in getting a book together. Asking a friend to do the illustrations is nearly always a waste of time. My friendly local artist is not necessarily able to illustrate picture books, which is a highly specialized skill, so I just send the story.

When the manuscript is ready and typed, double-spaced, without errors, on one side of the paper only, what next? One of the misconceptions I had about the practicalities of book production was the assumption that it would cost me a great deal to have a book published. The opposite is true. The only cost borne by the writer is the initial postage needed to send the story to a publisher. In the case of a picture-book manuscript, this should be little more than the cost of an ordinary letter plus the cost of a large, stamped, self-addressed envelope for the return of the manuscript, if necessary.

A copyright symbol © beside my name is both a precaution and a celebration of authorship, so I always use it. And I do try to remember to have a name, address, and telephone number on the bottom of the last page. (American publishers prefer it on the top of the first page.) Since each publishing house has its own particular "list" with its own peculiar tone, I use my own book collection and the advice of booksellers and librarians for advice on which publishers it would be most appropriate to approach with any given story.

The manuscript is of course accompanied by a covering letter that says something like this:

I Think I'll Write a Picture Book One Day . . .

Dear Editor,
*Enclosed is the manuscript for a picture book which I hope
you'll be kind enough to consider for publication.*
Yours sincerely, etc.

except that it's usually a more original and diverting variation
in order to reveal my "voice" and to attract the attention of
the jaded editor who's seen it all before, yawn, yawn. A reply
to this letter can take as long as eight to ten weeks—sometimes longer! If the story is rejected by one publisher—well,
there are many others. Rejection slips are still a regular humiliation in my life, but the only way to avoid them is not
to write. I can't remember exactly how many times *Koala
Lou* was rejected, but I know Omnibus refused it on the
grounds that they didn't want to get into an Australian-
animal rut, what with Kerry Argent's *One Woolly Wombat*
and my *Possum Magic.* The editor at Oxford University Press
rejected it, saying, "It doesn't quite work for me." Collins
rejected it. Hodder and Stoughton showed some interest,
but no contract after a year, and then Janine Day at Dent,
now at Ian Drakeford Publishing, took it, saying she loved
it. Of the twenty books I've published, the only ones that
weren't rejected at least once are this autobiography and
Wilfrid Gordon McDonald Partridge. I try to comfort myself
with the thought that the incredibly successful *Watership
Down* by Richard Adams was rejected by seventeen publishers
before it stormed its way into the bookshops.

Again and again my manuscripts are rejected by publishers who simply don't like the story as it is, in the manuscript
I've sent them. On the other hand, the blissful Jane Covernton at Omnibus took *Possum Magic,* not because it was

perfect but because it had potential. "You can write, Mem," said Jane, "and you have a story here somewhere. We'll just have to try and find it." (I used that line of hers later, in *Possum Magic.*) I admire the courage of editors who accept my writing because of the challenge of its potential.

After a story is accepted a contract arrives, eventually, and then an advance on the royalty, which is usually a minimum of $500. Having an agent means getting a much larger advance than that, because agents know how to haggle and aren't embarrassed to do so. The most likely terms to be offered, because they are the standard terms for picture books, are 5 percent of the profits from the recommended retail price. For example, if a book costs $15 in the shops, the writer receives 75 cents from each copy. The artist gets 75 cents also. Those so gifted as to be able both to draw and write their picture books would receive $1.50 per book sold. It may sound like peanuts, but if a book becomes a best-seller with sales of fifty thousand copies it becomes more than worthwhile in spite of the tax.

The publisher, the writer, and the artist are all equally creatively involved in producing the book. It isn't the writer's sole property, so throwing one's weight around is frowned upon. I've also learned that it's the artist's right to interpret the story as he or she thinks fit. I don't interfere, unless the artist requests it. Personally, I'm so visually inept that I don't see images as I write. In fact I don't think about the illustrations at all. In any case, a reputation for being temperamental about artwork would make publishers wary of dealing with me a second time. If I'm unhappy with the illustrations, that's too bad. There's very little that can be done about it, and that fact has to be accepted. Mostly I've been very lucky.

Among my illustrators there are many whom I've neither met nor spoken to, although I do love meeting them when the opportunity arises. It's fun to see if the illustrative style matches the person in real life. Putting a face to Terry Denton confirmed the hunches I'd had about him from his offbeat pictures for *Night Noises:* his limbs were long and loose, his shaggy multicolored sweater was long and loose, and his lovely friendly way of talking was also sort of long and loose.

Illustrators, once found, and depending on how busy they are, take six to eighteen months to finish the drawings or paintings. The illustrations for *Koala Lou* took Pam Lofts over a year to complete, but they were well worth waiting for: they're perfect reflections of the tenderness in my story and I love them. Vivienne Goodman took three years to do *Guess What?,* but that's because she paints with the genius and detail of a modern Australian Brueghel.

And finally, two to three years (or in the case of *Koala Lou,* five years and forty-nine drafts) after the first tentative scribbles find their way onto a blank page, six to ten free copies of the real thing arrive in the post. These are the only free copies that the writer ever receives. Even with a 40 percent writer's discount, providing copies for friends and family isn't cheap.

After publication, there are always the reviews to be faced. I can't explain why, but good reviews go in one eye and out the other, whereas bad reviews seem to pollute my memory forever. I've had lukewarm reviews for books that have gone on to become best-sellers, but that's no comfort at the time. I nearly wept over this review of the extraordinary *Guess What?:*

Placing this book into an age category is extremely difficult. Like books such as Animalia *it will find its own level, or levels, for it will appeal differently to different ages. Basically the problem is that it has a weak, rather banal text, of the predictable type and one that does not make for exciting, repeated read aloud sessions. The illustrations are, however, stunning to look at and highly sophisticated. It is as though the writer and the artist have different audiences in mind.*

The story (?) is a series of questions about Daisy O'Grady and the reader is asked to guess what she may look like. Bit by bit is built up an image of the woman, although the astute reader knows what she is long before the end.

There will, though, be those readers who may find the content disturbing, for some pages tend to be a little frightening; others will be delighted with the comic elements in them. Vivienne Goodman is certainly a talent who is sure to go a long way.

(Magpies No. 3, July 1988.)

The self-exposure inherent in being published invites such barbs, but they always hurt no matter how brave a face one puts on it. Who'd risk writing another picture book after a review like that, especially if she'd taken enormous care, as I had done, to *ensure* that the text was sufficiently predictable for very young readers? Are reviewers of children's books unaware of the innovations in the teaching of reading? It would seem so. But the reviewer was right about the illustrations: they're the most bizarre and exciting pictures in any of my books. I'm crazy about them.

Even worse than the *Guess What?* review was the one for the miniature *Possum Magic* in *Reading Time* in 1987, after the publication of reprint after reprint of the normal-size edition. The text of the minibook was exactly the same as in the original version; only the size had changed. Nevertheless, a reviewer found it possible to write:

> Vivas's delightful ink and wash drawings bring out the soft and endearing qualities of the Australian bush characters. Mem Fox achieves moments of cleverness and humour in the text but she strives to be Australian at all costs. This detracts from the plot and weakens the story. I found, on re-reading the story some years later, that I had been hooked by the enchanting illustrations and had overlooked the flaws in the text.

Well, well, you don't say! I was terribly upset. On the day that it appeared I made a long-distance distress call to a friend in Brisbane, Joan Zahnleiter, who's an experienced reviewer of children's literature, hoping she'd say, "There, there. Don't get into such a state. It's laughable!" And, thank God, she did. How writers can claim not to read reviews or claim to be immune to them is beyond my comprehension.

Fortunately, beyond these reviews lies the comforting compensation of royalty checks. After six to twelve months of sales, Australian royalties are paid twice a year, usually on March 31 for sales from July to December, and on September 30 for sales from January to June. (American royalties are paid in a similar fashion.) As a writer, the sale of overseas rights is barely of interest to me, since reduced royalty rates apply and the returns are comparatively small. Eleven of my books have been published in America, for instance, but in financial terms the excitement over being published in the United States or the U.K. is often misplaced. One of my books, *With Love at Christmas,* is published only in the U.S.A. (having been deemed too religious for the Australian market) so the more normal 5 percent applies in that particular case, since no sale of rights has occurred between countries.

The advantage of being published overseas is in the exposure of one's books and, if one feels so inclined, of oneself. Americans are enormously generous in their admiration of writers, in their organization of writers' tours, and in their care of writers. In America my publishers send me on tour with a minder, and sometimes even with two, who see to my every need. I don't have to carry my bags, nor do I have to check into hotels, or stand in line in airports, or sleep in anything other than first-class hotels. As an Australian writer of children's fiction, who am I to resist star treatment if it's offered, from time to time? Having said that, however, on an exhausting three-week tour, working daily with no weekends off, from 8:00 A.M. until 10:30 P.M., I need two minders to pick up the pieces on the occasions when things fall apart.

Once a writer has had a success or two and feels that a literary agent might be useful as a guide and protector in the publishing world, he or she has only to write to one to ask to be taken on. There are, however, very few literary agents in Australia and as far as I know they all work from either

Melbourne or Sydney. Agents normally take 10 percent of one's royalties, but it's well worth it in my opinion—and with my particular agent—for the freedom from stress it provides.

I hope this chapter proves to be useful to those who have the inclination and time to write a picture book, as well as the concomitant tenacity, temerity, and typewriter. Contrary to popular belief, ignorance is not bliss. Bliss is being published. I wish someone had told me what I now know before I stepped out so jauntily along my hopeful road, blind to the potholes and deaf to the dangers and difficulties of wanting to be a picture-book writer. Small wonder that I now feel murderous when I experience the condescension of those who say, "I think I'll write a picture book one day when I have the time." So! Is time all it takes? Hmmmm. It's an unwitting insult to those of us who've had a picture book published and nearly died in the attempt. It makes us dangerous at dinner parties and pugilistic in public. Whereas, a novel! Well! I think I'll write a novel one day—when I have the time . . .

16

Writing: Methods, Madness, and Material

Roald Dahl, so I've heard, wrote in a little shed in his back garden that, according to the folklore, had been cleaned only once, after a goat found its way inside and left droppings on the floor. Fay Weldon, I believe, writes her novels at the kitchen table among the clamor of her children. In neither environment would I be capable of writing a word. I'm so fastidious and lacking in concentration that I need solitude, silence, and a clean and tidy work space before I begin.

The house we live in, which I love, had only two bedrooms and a study when we moved in. Malcolm and I thought we'd share the study. Ha. I found myself increasingly at the kitchen table because I couldn't work in his mess. After *Possum Magic* we extended the house, making it half as big again. Included in these extensions was my study. Such was their expense that Malcolm tells the world he locks me in every night and calls through the keyhole, "How much have you written? Will it pay for the extensions?"

My desk is narrow and eight feet long. I designed it myself. On this desk, among the usual paraphernalia, are certain essential items peculiar to my neurotic needs. I write in pencil, using soft-lead pencils always, since the softness means not having to press hard on the paper. As I write, charging along with thoughts that seem to be falling exactly into place, it's maddening to have to stop and sharpen a pencil, so there's an average of thirty pencils in my pencil pot, varying in length from stubs to brand-new. Pencils necessitate sharpeners, so there are three of those, as well as a couple of erasers. Because I make frequent changes by rubbing out the rubbish I've written, a gray snow of rubber crumbs eventually litters my writing area. Fastidious as ever, I sweep them away regularly with a blue baby's brush bought specifically for the purpose. Scissors and tape are also among my essentials, since how can one cut and paste without them? Also on the desk are an inadequate *Concise Oxford Dictionary*, a brand-new *Roget's Thesaurus* (the first copy I owned has fallen apart), a tattered *Penguin Dictionary of Quotations*, and a battered copy of Strunk and White's *Elements of Style*. With these tools and a pad of lined paper I am physically well equipped to write my first sentence.

In every situation, no matter what the genre, that first sentence is the hardest. Because the beginning of a piece is a signpost to its tone and content I usually can't continue

163

until it's hammered into place. Here's the first line of the first draft of *Koala Blue and the Bush Olympics*, written on a scrap of paper on August 29, 1983:

> *Beyond the back of Bourke but not very far from the*
> *Black Stump lived Koala Blue and Kookaburra Brown.*

Clearly I was still locked in the rah-rah-Australiah mode in which I'd written *Possum Magic*. But a week later the beginning of the second draft had already been changed to:

> *Not in this time, nor in that time, but in one particular*
> *time, a bush fire blackened everything from way up*
> *north to way out west.*

I was writing in 1983, the year of horrific bush fires in Victoria and South Australia. This beginning, borrowed from Iranian storytelling tradition, remained until draft thirteen on September 17. Underneath draft thirteen I wrote, "Lucky last?" Of course it wasn't. There were another thirty-six after that, and who finally wrote the best beginning? The beginning as it's published today? Me? Heavens, no! It was my editor, Janine Day:

> *There was once a baby koala so soft and round that*
> *all who saw her loved her. Her name was Koala Lou.*

Perfect rhythm. See why I hate writing picture books? Half the lines aren't even mine. In *Possum Magic* Malcolm suggested "Mornay and Minties in Melbourne," and Celia Jellet, one of the Omnibus editors, suggested "Pumpkin scones in

Brisbane." Gillian Rubinstein, a well-known and controversial writer for children, wrote the ending of *Night Noises*, and my Malcolm supplied the last line of *Feathers and Fools*. Thank Heaven they don't ask for royalties.

I write in silence although I have a tape recorder on my desk and rows of tapes to choose from. Bach is my favorite, but he's only given permission to fill the room when I'm pottering about, because writing for me is like composing, and I find it impossible to compose if someone else's music is playing at the same time. A blowfly will so disrupt my concentration that I can't continue until I've killed it. In picture books, particularly, the choice of words is as crucial as the choice of notes in a fugue. I constantly read aloud what I've written in order to feel and hear the rightness of phrases or sentences. I know from experience that a rhythm that seems fine on the silent page often turns out to be clumsy or unwieldy when it's spoken.

One of the reasons I find picture books so difficult is because of my exposure to the Bible and Shakespeare. On one hand it's an advantage. It means I have a deep understanding of the sound and the feel of the English language. On the other hand, it's maddening because I myself, personally, as they say, am not actually William Shakespeare, a fact that frustrates me every time I sit at my desk. Shakespeare gets the rhythm right every time. Why then, oh, why can't I? Most of the drafts of *Koala Lou* focused on the problem of rhythm. I spent whole days working on single sentences, reading them aloud, rewriting them, and reading them aloud again. To use another musical analogy, I could hear the tunes in my head, but I couldn't sing them onto the paper. It drove me mad.

I don't know, before I start, quite how an article or a chapter will develop, nor how a book will blossom. I never make an outline. For me an outline is like a straitjacket that prevents me from being creative, divergent. The narrow confines of a picture book are bad enough already. There's no room to move. Its text is akin to a sonnet: small, powerful, and tightly disciplined. It's like a short, smooth plank when seen beside the luxuriant oak-tree effect of a novel. I don't even make early or rigid decisions about content although I am dimly aware of the theme and plot of a picture book before I begin, and of the subject I'll be attempting to explore in any given article.

When I've finally drawn a line under the last sentence of a much-rewritten first draft (the last line can take days to perfect since the balance of its phrasing is, for me, so painfully difficult to achieve) I have my piece typed onto our word processor, which is not in my study but just outside it, in case others need to use it. I make multiple copies and ask for reactions to my newly completed opus from Malcolm and other selected friends. If I didn't talk about my writing, how would I know what to improve? In fact, rewriting is often synonymous with retalking to anyone who'll listen. When I didn't have any times recorded for Koala Klaws's rapid climb to the top of the tree, a Year Seven class in Brighton, South Australia, asked, "How fast was Koala Klaws? And how high did she climb?" Until then I hadn't thought about it, nor had I realized that anyone would be interested.

Mind you, I don't like the readers who react to my writing in any but glowing terms. Truly, I can't stand them! Their monstrous comments, their lofty criticism, their lack of energetic and unqualified praise of my work make my throat tighten as I wonder, amazed, how I could call them my *friends*. I seethe over negative feedback. Years of experience haven't altered my behavior. What has changed, however, is an acceptance of my attitude in these circumstances. Although I plead for reactions because I need them in order to improve what I've written, I know I'll loathe the people who criticize a single word, let alone the tone or structure. I allow myself to simmer with rage. I allow myself to deny that my so-called *friends* have any editorial talent whatsoever. I allow myself to believe that what they have said couldn't possibly be true, damn them.

Eventually, when the lid on my fury has stopped rattling and I'm calm enough to return to a state of objectivity, I realize, chastened, the validity of many of their remarks and return to the computer to press the delete button. Rewriting on a word processor is a dream compared to hand-writing, although I'm quite unable to write a first draft on it. On the occasions when I've tried, my style changes to short sentences that are too smart by half, and acutely overwritten. The pencil and I are essential mates in the consummation of my "literary works."

Not everything I write is a "literary work." I've said that I can't bear the process involved in writing picture books, but I do love writing letters, especially to people who expect formality and receive, from me, a naughty informality designed to cheer them up. It's fun to begin a letter with "My darling bureaucrat" instead of "Dear Sir." It was fun to be wicked with Alan Bond, who launched *Sail Away*, and tongue-in-cheek with Hazel Hawke, who launched the deaf

version of *Arabella*. It was fun also to write to the architect
of our extensions, towards the end of the building project:

Dear Brian,

*Here I am, home again, and eager to bring The Extension
Situation to a close. The State Bank is satisfied with the work
and will pay the builder as soon as we indicate in writing that
we are similarly satisfied. A few things still require attention,
however.*

*1.   There are still no handles on the drawers in my office.
This is, as you can imagine, an extreme hazard to my nails!*

*2.   The toilet seat is so badly positioned that it will not
stay up. I fear the intimate danger this may cause any male
guest. . . .*

*3.   The bricks on the patio have not been replaced and, as
it is unlikely that we shall excavate for buried treasure in the
near future, I would like them replaced as soon as possible.*

*4.   Although we do not see eye to eye with our neighbor (he
is very short), I would be unhappy to see him killed by falling
bricks when he leans over the fence to gasp in admiration at
our extensions. The brick wall separating our properties could,
at present, be pushed over by a child. The damage to the wall
was caused during the initial excavations. Early rectification
of this danger would be appreciated.*

*5.   Otherwise the place is a perfection of taste and
convenience—thank you! I love it.*

*The State Bank mentioned that the builder was expecting
all the rest of the money. I was puzzled because I understood
that we would save approximately $2,000 by not having a
retaining wall built. I have exquisitely good eyesight and search
though I might, I cannot find a retaining wall! I hope that*

you can clarify this situation. I'm a writer, not a mathematician.

With happy thanks,
Mem Fox

I write to please myself, and to tickle the fancy of my readers. When a local feminist bookshop called The Murphy Sisters celebrated its fifth birthday, I bought a card but stood in the post office unable to seal it until I'd put my own metaphorical stamp on it. I wanted to write a pertinent little verse, but all I could think of was "The boy stood on the burning deck. . . ." I couldn't use *boy* for a feminist bookshop so I tried *girl* instead, and the rest followed:

> *The girl stood on the burning deck,*
> *Her feet were full of blisters.*
> *She could not move—*
> *Her head was in*
> *A book from Murphy Sisters!*

The adage "Why should I write if I know what I'm going to say?" has stood me in good stead. I've been astounded frequently by the insights I've been able to gain about a particular subject simply by reflecting on the page or paragraph just written, yet it was only as a mature-age student of English at university that I discovered one could write to learn. Prior to that I'd thought that writing in the context of education was to prove that one *had* learned.

When I'm putting together an academic paper an idea can mull around in my head for three months before I begin organizing my thoughts on paper, and then it can take weeks

169

of hard yakka to shape it into something useful, pleasing, and easy to read. On one hand it's incredibly demanding, but on the other it provides a perverse sort of enjoyment: *having written* feels marvelous. I particularly enjoyed writing two papers, "The Fox in Possum's Clothing: a teacher disguised as writer, in hot pursuit of literacy" (*Language Arts*, Vol. 64. No. 1, January 1987) and "Notes from the Battlefield: towards a theory of why people write" (*Language Arts*, Vol. 65. No. 2, February 1988), because as I wrote, I was discovering what I didn't know I knew about the links between writing and reading. I was so consumed by them that the rest of my daily life seemed an irritation, an irrelevance.

Nonacademic articles can be the wildest fun to write but are just as hard to get right as the academic pieces. For example, I redrafted for months my *Adelaide Review* piece (May '89) in praise of state schooling and private-education-through-travel, whose subtitle was "Why my heiress went to the local high school." I knew I was treading through a war-zone of opposing and dearly held opinions so I rewrote meticulously in order to create simultaneously the maximum impact, the least offense, and the lightest possible tone. Writing that seems merely to have slipped from my pen onto the page has nearly always been dug over and recomposted, with patience, for weeks. The lighter the tone, the harder the work.

Tone was my greatest stumbling block in writing the regular Wombat Book Club newsletters for the Ashton Scholastic publishing house in 1986/7. The book club was aimed at preschoolers. I had to write for their parents, who were, I presumed, everything from highly privileged to down-and-out. My brief was to write cheerfully, not to be pompous or patronizing, not to use jargon, and yet to say something worthwhile about parents' roles in early literacy development. In my head I invented a professor (female) and a teenage single mother whom I sat on either side of me. Then I wrote, in a kind of agony, trying to please them both.

Whenever there's nothing I have to write I look for something I'd like to write. I love writing, so long as it's not picture books. From the age of seventeen onwards I've been an intermittent journal writer. The earliest journal extant is the single book I filled during my three years at drama school, from '65 to '68. I didn't keep a journal again until 1981, when I retrained in language arts and was encouraged to keep one as a daily discipline, but the "daily" element didn't last. However, in 1984, because of George Orwell's unfulfilled predictions in his book *Nineteen Eighty-Four*, I decided to write in my journal every day no matter how tired or pressed for time I was. It wore me out and I vowed never to do it again, but I was inspired by the Australian Bicentenary and weakened in 1988. My character is such that if I set out to do something I won't give in until I've done it, which is why I wrote in my journal every day that year, in spite of being phenomenally busy.

The twenty-seven journals I have now filled (most have black covers and red bindings) are examples of the sort of drivel people write when they know the audience isn't important. The picture painted in my journals is that of a fraught woman obsessed with perfection in every facet of her life, usually tired, either in ecstasy or in despair, but rarely calmly balanced. I find my journals shocking because they're a mirror in which I see a disturbing vision of myself, so I don't read them often.

171

My most regular piece of unliterary work is the letter I write to my parents every Sunday. For twenty-six years I have maintained this weekly habit, happy to keep in touch, longing for the loving reactions and news that I receive in return. I've been in some wonderful places on the Sundays of my life, from Greek hovels and Danish red-light districts (by mistake) to American airports and Fijian beaches, but I've always made time for my letter "home." It's partly due to the fanaticism of my character, of course, as well as to the fact that my parents are lovely people who appreciate and reciprocate the communication. Letters home are pleasant "little pieces," easy to write and easy to enjoy, one of my favorite forms of relaxation. It's like searching for handkerchiefs to iron when I'm sick of ironing my shirts. (Malcolm irons his own shirts in the cruelly liberated world in which he now finds himself.)

I write mostly late at night, often until two A.M. Or at weekends. I write when I'm not teaching, shopping, cleaning, tidying, chatting to Chloë and Malcolm, seeing friends, cooking, traveling, watching films, promoting books, ironing, answering kids' letters, marking, listening to Bach, preparing classes, reading novels, making beds, or inhaling Ventolin.

My output of twenty books in seven years perplexes me, since I can't remember when I found the time to do them. In the madness of my days I have little recollection of writing any books at all, other than *Possum Magic* and *Koala Lou*, but there they are, the Collected Works, sitting upright and pleased with themselves on my shelf: evidence of silent moments snatched from a noisy life as I lived on, clattering ever after.

17

Dear Mem

Dear Mem,
Wilfrid Gordon McDonald Partridge *is a verey love book. My teacher read it to us. I think it will win first present in Book Week.* . . .

Dear Mem Fox,
I love your books because they make sense. I love Goodnight Sleep Tight
From Alexandra

Dear Mem Fox,
I have read all your books even the pathetic ones. . . .

Dear Ms Fox

I liked Shoe's from Grandpa *because nerly every word rimed. I'm amased how such A Person coude rite a story like that. I wish I could rite a story like that and I wish I was a story riter. and just a reminda if enyone calle's you a silly story riter tell them that a howll class likes you.*

Love Christian.

Dear Mem Fox,

My name is Simon. I'am five 5 I go to scheel it is fun I'am nele six 6 I like Gess Wott

Dear Mem Fox,

Thank you for coming. The story you mad up it was a funny story. You are a nice liade. Your hair looks nice. What do you put in your hair.

Love, Denise.

These, and other delightful letters like them, arrive in great numbers each week, brightening my days and occupying my nights. Being a letter writer myself, I know how important it is for children—and others—to receive a reply as soon as possible. I do my best. I reply to each one, usually within three weeks, which means increasingly that letters have become the bane of my life. I love reading them. The problem is finding the time to reply.

One Sunday night in late '86 I sat at my desk for nearly five hours answering twenty-six letters from children, friends, publishers, family, teachers, and librarians. When I'd finished I thought, "Thank God! At last I'm up to date." But the next day when I went down the drive to clear the mail-

174

box, I found another six letters written in kids' handwriting. I leaned against the garden wall, depressed. On the back of one of the envelopes was written, "*Sail away* IS ACE!!!" *Sail Away* had just been published. I realized that the letters would never stop, and that with every new book it would get worse. And it did. There were so many books in the pipeline. I wondered how I'd be able to cope with my correspondence on top of the already heavy evening work associated with my teaching. Panic set in when letters began to arrive from the U.S.A. with its vast population of young readers. Cost, as well as time, began to be a consideration. So this was the price of fame!

No two children write quite the same letter, I've discovered, so a form letter in reply has proved to be impossible. Each answer turns out to be original and personal, sometimes handwritten, but more often dictated for typing in order to save my hand and wrist. I suffer genuinely from writer's cramp. In order to maintain my enthusiasm for the task I keep a picture in my mind of the children I'm writing to, imagining their reaction as my letters are read. I always hope they'll be thrilled.

I'd be mortified if children were ever able to guess how hard it is to find the time and energy to reply to their letters, so I write back cheerfully, in a loud voice as it were, bubbling with excitement over their reactions to my books even though I've read similar reactions many times before. It isn't only my Protestant work ethic that urges me to behave with such sickening dedication, it's also my understanding as a teacher of the importance of encouraging children to read and write for real rewards. I'd hate to be the one who put them off.

For this reason I'm bothered by the letters from kids who write and say, "I have to write to an author for a school assignment so I'm writing to you." I feel like writing back and saying, "Well, I don't *have* to write to anyone, my darling, so I'm not writing back to you!" Of course I don't, but I do feel unhappy about letters from children who have to write to authors in case it makes them hate writing, and hate books—mine, in particular. Allowing or encouraging children to write to authors is a terrific idea, but I think compelling them to do so is of questionable value.

I worry also about the letters from children who ask me to send them one of my books. Contrary to popular belief and as I've already said, writers aren't provided with endless free copies of their books, so sending books is impossible, and therefore disappointing for the child who asked in the first place. Photos are easier to provide, but even those aren't free. The mere cost of a stamp is more than half the average royalty on a picture book.

On the whole, teachers and librarians are wonderfully understanding when it comes to letters to authors, and there's rarely a request for a reply that I don't happily grant. "If possible . . . ," they say. "If you could find the time . . ." And all the letters from one class are either in a single envelope or at least posted on the same day, so that thirty letters from one school don't arrive in dribs and drabs over weeks, thereby making it hard to write a whole-class letter in reply. I once had so many letters from a school called Our Lady Help of Christians, arriving in ones and twos over what seemed like months, that I thought I'd need the help of Christians myself before it was all over.

Occasionally there's a blunt, pro forma letter that has

clearly been sent to a number of writers without a thought for the agitated recipient on the other end, like this one:

To whom it may concern:

Please find enclosed a letter from junior primary students. We would be pleased if you could reply to this letter as soon as possible, as students are awaiting responses for their schoolwork.

Thank you for your help.
                                        Yours faithfully,

There was no "Dear Mem," and the letter wasn't even signed. Instead there was a photocopied signature. The assumption that the children had a deadline, but that I would have no such deadlines in my own life, was an affront, and I was so stressed at the time that I actually cried over this letter. There was also an assumption that I would not answer as soon as I possibly could, whereas the reverse is true. I answer as soon as I can.

Letters such as these upset me enormously and tend to slow down my reply since I can't write until I've stopped sulking. It's like the "P.S. Please write soon" on many children's letters, except that in the case of children it's less of a real request, I believe, than a letter-writing convention similar to writing "THE END" at the end of a story.

Receiving a stamped, addressed envelope for a reply isn't very common, but it's always welcome, even though the envelope is usually too small to contain the information requested. In these cases I pry the stamp off the standard envelope provided and reglue it onto an envelope big enough to send back the fat questionnaire that was sent in the first place. Loose stamps are best. I swoop on them in delight. They're a godsend, since they can be used for anything.

The cleverness of children's invented spelling is a constant treat as Malcolm, Chloë, and I sit at the kitchen table deciphering piles of letters together, reading them aloud, loving the words, in hysterics over the things kids say. Sometimes we can tell by the "accent" of the invented spelling whether the letter has come from Australia or America. This one is from America, followed by its translation:

Dear Mem

We mos you. I love your tape. I mess you a lot. I licke your books Pasahm Mahjak and Hadeiy and the Fox and Wath Love at Crasiemase. I hop you oar dowing fan.

Love Suzanne.

(Dear Mem,

We miss you. I love your tape. I miss you a lot. I like your books Possum Magic *and* Hattie and the Fox *and* With Love at Christmas. *I hope you are doing fine.*

Love,

Suzanne)

In that letter we thought we could even detect that the accent was southern U.S.A. from the "you oar dowing fan," and we were right. It was from Florida. The one that follows is Australian, as evidenced by the "finke" instead of *thing* in the last line:

Dear Mem

Dear Mem,
I like your storre very muth. I like haw you rit your storre. There nis storre. I like haw you tork and yor nis and I love you very muth love from Evie xxxooooxxx I love you very muth. I like the books. I like the books very muth and I like all ov you. I like yor clos very muth. I like efry finke.

(Dear Mem,
I like your story very much. I like how you write your story. They're nice stories. I like how you talk and you're nice. I love you very much   love from Evie xxxooooxxx I love you very much. I like the books very much and I like all of you. I like your clothes very much. I like everything.)

I admire in particular the way children write using the *sound* of a letter sometimes and the *name* of a letter at others, as in "huh, oh, puh" which makes "hop" into "hope." In the same way "rit" becomes "write," "nis" becomes "nice," and "lik" becomes "like." Lots of children declare that they lik my books, poor things. I hop they taste nis.

There are lots of questions about my name, which is my real name after all and not a pseudonym, even though it isn't exactly what I was christened. My favorite letter on this subject was from Western Australia:

Dear Mem Fox,
Thank you for writing Possum Magic, Sail Away The ballad of Skip and Nell, *and* Wilfrid Gordon McDonald Partridge. *Mem fox wot is your rill name.*
From Leonie

179

Names! Often there's no surname on the bottom of a letter and I have to address the reply merely to Kerry or Wayne. I presume the letter arrives eventually. What's worse is when the writer's address is written not on the letter (Oh, would that it were!), but only on the back of the envelope. I open my letters and read them and put them in a pile on the table. The envelopes get thrown in the bin. When the time comes to answer the letters I find I've thrown away some of the addresses, which means that I have to unwrap plastic bags of rubbish and feel through heaven-knows-what revolting garbage to find them. Then I have to try to match the letter to its envelope. Addresses on letters would solve the problem.

There's more joy than woe, however:

Dear Mem Fox,

We really don't know what name to call you. Do you like Mem Fox or just Mem or Miss Storyteller or Miss Mem or Mrs Fox. Any way we would like to tell you we loved all your stories. Can you please tell us how you think up the names for your stories and how many stories have you written? (It must be millions there everywhere in the school.) This week we made some jelly. Can you guess what colorur. You're right—red. Here is a jelly joke for you. How do you start a jelly race?

GET SET
Love from IR
xxooo

180

Dear Mem

Dear Mem fox, it was a pleasure for having you. I hop you have a good trip. thank you for speding your pearshes time. I which you cod stay longer to. Boy ho! From Kassy.

Lastly—and cruelly:

Dear Mem Fox, I bet when you were young you were pretty and fun to be with!!!

I love children's letters. Most of the time.

18

Wearing the Other Hat

I may be keen on writing, but the real passion of my life is teaching. In class, just being there keeps the adrenaline going. It would be an exaggeration to say that I love all my students, and an overstatement to declare that they all love me—I can be terrifying and even unreasonable—but on the whole we're a lively bunch of people who have an exciting and rewarding time together.

By choice, at the moment I teach two compulsory courses to the 150 First Years who want to be teachers. They range in age from straight-from-school to prime-of-life: forty-five, like me. In the first semester these would-be teachers relearn how to speak and write with confidence, effectiveness, correctness, and liveliness. In the second semester I teach the teaching of reading and writing, speaking and listening.

I take teaching and learning very seriously, but I'm rarely serious in the act of teaching. One of my better-remembered efforts was a lecture on stealing from other writers. The point I wanted to make was that writers learn most about writing from reading. Other people's writing influences and teaches, inspires and refreshes. I wanted my students to realize how essential it is to read aloud to children, and how important it is for anyone to read in order to become a better writer.

It was a compulsory lecture at nine o'clock on a Monday morning. I entered shamefaced, handcuffed to a real policeman. I had written permission to do this from the police commissioner himself. The buzz of talk among the students suddenly stopped. My heart pounded as the policeman said, "Does anyone here recognize this woman?"

"Ye-es," came a chorus of replies.

"Well, I'm here to inform you that she's just been arrested on a charge of larceny. She stands accused of stealing from other writers. She'll be appearing in court later this morning. I believe she had a prior engagement with you, so I'm allowing her one hour to explain her actions."

He unclipped the handcuffs and strode to the doors at the top of the room, where he sat, his arms folded grimly.

I used the hour to unpack the evidence, from my own writing, of how useful it is for writers to read. I presented the exhibits, a small number of them, from among my load of stolen goods: the rhyme scheme and the setting grabbed unconsciously from *The Rime of the Ancient Mariner* to use in my *Sail Away*; the last line of *Possum Magic*, "And she did," nicked quietly from the story of *The Little Red Hen;* a couple of phrases—"Now it came to pass" and "in peace and unafraid"—in *Feathers and Fools,* whipped straight from the Bible; the underlying theme of Pat Hutchins's *Rosie's Walk* lifted unwittingly for my *Hattie and the Fox,* and so on.

At the end of the lecture the students clapped and cheered as the solemn policeman rearrested me. He and I didn't laugh until we were well outside. His handcuffs kept me from floating to the seventh heaven. I'm potty about teaching.

In another lecture I dimmed the lighting and entered wearing a long white nightdress. Moving from student to student with a candle in my hand, I recited night poems: anything from "Wee Willie Winkie" to Herrick's "The Night-Piece, to Julia." Once I'd caught the students' attention I turned on the lights and got on with the business of the lecture—the importance of reading poetry to children. Planning the medium of my message always takes longer than the delivery of it.

I prefer workshops to lectures because the learning is so much more active. In my lectures no one would dream of talking, but in my workshops few would dream of not talking. Writing workshops are my favorite. The class and I toss topics to and fro, wondering what to write about. The noise level rises and falls. Suggestions bounce around the group. Occasionally I guffaw. We are enjoying each other's company. Then there's silence. Everyone, including me, writes.

Ten minutes pass. Glancing at the piece being written by the student to my right, I suddenly leap to my feet, yelling in triumph. I kiss him deliriously on both cheeks and call him a clever little fart-face, or worse. (The alliteration turns it into an endearment.) He has written the word *definitely* correctly for the first time in his life, although he's nearly nineteen and hopes to be a teacher.

"Read your piece to us," I say. "I'm ecstatic about the spelling, but the subject you're writing about is even more interesting."

We sit at the feet of the writer. His paper trembles. He reads a piece called "Leaving Home," and we discover how terribly homesick he is for his family, back on the farm, and how lonely he is. I'm not the only one who is moved.

In those sessions in which each of us reads our writing to the class we shake with nerves, knowing that our naked talent is about to be exposed for all to hear. As one student put it: "This year is the first time I've written not for a grade, but for people." We laugh at some pieces till we're half slid from our seats, and fumble for tissues during others. When I'm asked why I love teaching, I'm tongue-tied: "Because I love the atmosphere in my classes" sounds peculiarly inconsequential.

The worst of times for any teacher is surely assessment. Because I want my students to be the best possible teachers my standards are high. It's rumored that a misplaced comma, a forgotten question mark, inept quotation marks, or a single spelling error will cause them to fail. The rumor is only slightly exaggerated.

Often the standards of spelling, punctuation, and grammar, and the thought-and-structure elements of my students' writing, are so dire as to emotionally exhaust me. Somewhere along the way they've stopped caring because some of their previous teachers haven't cared, because they haven't seen the colossal need to care. This ill-treatment has rendered them powerless as writers and therefore powerless as people. It's their powerlessness as people that upsets me most.

I respond to my students' work on an audiotape, which they provide. In the privacy of a personal chat I can respond at length to what each one has written, or tried to write. I can ask questions, laugh, sympathize, compare my own experience, make suggestions, be angry, or be fulsome in my praise. I can send silly messages to the student's family: "Call your mum into your room—I want to talk to her about the naughtiness of your apostrophes. She can beat you. I'm not allowed to."

At the end of first semester tape recorders are begged, borrowed, and overused in the corridors and in the cafeteria. Some students rush to their cars to plug in their tapes in privacy. Others, impatient, listen outside my office. "Ssh. Ssh. I can't hear. Oh, my God, Mem's such a whacker! Listen to this. No, wait! Did I pass? Ssh. Ssh. I can't hear."

I love the intimacy of these taped conversations and find it useful to be able to teach, as it were, one-to-one, even though it takes countless hours. Conscientious mature-age students keep the comments so they can refer to my hints when they write their second-semester assignments. The young ones, grinning, say they'll sell them when I'm famous.

Practicing what I preach, I read aloud to my classes in every session. The more literature my students hear or read for pleasure, the less necessary it becomes to pick it apart in tedious explanation. The more they hear, the more they understand. For the disaffected, uncultured, and uninterested student, analysis is the rope by which literature hangs until it's dead. Usually only those who already enjoy prose and poetry benefit from or are interested in the finer points of interpretation, which so excite me.

In the writing course I include storytelling, reading aloud, choral speaking, and individual verse speaking. Each student learns a poem of his or her choice to recite by heart to an attentive and supportive class that sighs, and laughs, and listens, in spite of the fact that sitting through three hours of nonstop poetry is a new and dreaded experience. The verse speakers vary from introverted music students to extroverted League footballers.

"What, me? Poetry? You must be joking!"

But I'm not. Everyone does it and everyone succeeds to the best of his or her memory, although some seem likely to faint with the strain and are only revived by tumultuous applause from their mates and me.

My reputation as a writer holds no water among my students. They know about it because I mention it so often. Too often. Although their children or little brothers and sisters might be pleased that the author of *Possum Magic* is teaching one of the family, the students themselves couldn't care less. If I weren't safely protected from the lionizing I experience outside the college by the lack of lionizing I experience within the college, I might have lost my head. Teaching keeps me humble. Well, *moderately* humble.

In trying to define my satisfaction as a teacher, I've begun to realize that my enjoyment owes much to the relationship between my learners and me in the bubbling hyperactivity of our classes. The long-term togetherness is what I love: getting to know people, caring for them, knocking them into shape, watching them develop, swapping gossip. Although

I demand a high level of commitment in return for my own work and enthusiasm, the students don't seem to mind. They're very warm and friendly.

If I observe any loss of interest in class I blame myself. My eyes are everywhere, alert for lack of engagement, pouncing on it with a shocking laugh and a worse expletive, jolting students from stupor to attention, from detachment to activity. As I survey the wondrous chaos, as I observe the learning that's taking place and listen to the shouting and the laughter, I know I could never give up teaching. I'd go into a decline, aching for the noisy zip-zap of my classes.

Because I set myself up as a relaxed yet informed fool, making myself as approachable as I can, I live in hope that students will like me and love learning. But it doesn't always work. I know I've destroyed some of them by being too hard on them, or by setting expectations that are too high, or by frightening them with my loud and forceful personality. I can't bear to believe that I've ever failed as a teacher, but I have.

If it were possible to be the perfect teacher, I'd want to be it. I'd like to be a lasting and positive presence in the lives of all my students. I'd like to make an impact on them that cheers them on dull days, inspires them on clear days, and makes them ache with caring over the art of teaching all the days of their lives, even forevermore. And on that biblical note it might be as well to remember the illuminating graffiti scratched onto the wall of the third floor men's toilets at the Sturt campus: "Mem Fox is not God."

19

Tub-thumping

I may not be God but I certainly preach my own kind of gospel according to modern educational theory. I have espoused with fervor the beliefs of the "whole language" movement whose methods of teaching reading and writing are both life-enhancing and highly successful.

"Whole language" has caught me up and will not let me go, in much the same way that Africa caught my parents up and would not let *them* go. I've become a different kind of missionary in my own field, fired with zeal about exciting new ways of teaching reading and writing in our schools and colleges. As I travel Australia and America I'm amused to find I have to stop myself from thumping each podium as if it were a pulpit.

In the United States, I have discovered, there appears to be some confusion about the precise meaning of "whole language." For me, the confusion has been useful since it has caused me to rethink and to redefine my terms.

The term "whole language" arose when it became necessary to describe a new way of teaching reading and writing in relation to the old way. It has become so open to abuse and misunderstanding I now prefer to use the term "real language," since that's what "whole language" means.

The old way of teaching reading and writing is probably best remembered by people like me who learned to read long before the 1980s. We learned to read and write in parts, in bits, not in whole meanings.

For example, we used to learn lists of single, yet similar, words like *bat, cat, hat, mat, sat,* and *that,* and *bough, dough, rough, trough,* and *though.* These lists would often appear on charts that decorated our classroom walls or hung from the ceilings on string, disconnected from the reality of our lives, divorced from sentences, and therefore devoid of immediate meaning. Single, unconnected words on flashcards would be held up for us to recognize, and we would chant them aloud, believing that we were learning to read. Indeed, many of us did learn to read by this method, but too many did not.

The boring, unrewarding, unreal schoolbooks we then had to struggle through—about Dick and Dora, John and Betty—turned many children off reading within a few months of arriving at school. "If this is reading," they must have thought, "why would anyone bother to read?" Basal readers were, and remain, emotional deserts between two covers. Little children who stagger across the arid vocabulary towards an elusive literacy often collapse along the way, thirsting for the language of life. They find themselves instead surrounded by death: a dead plot here, a dead theme there; a dead tone, dead setting, dead character—everywhere a dead style.

It is, I believe, quite dreadful to write books, or to use books, even basal readers, in order to teach merely the *mechanics* of reading (rather than the *love* of reading), yet publishers print vast quantities of these profitable, execrable texts every year. This basal-reader overkill has given rise to millions of adult illiterates who daily shame their nations and daily shame themselves. It seems clear to me that in the teaching of reading we ought to phase out the use of basal readers as soon as possible and use real books instead.

Real books (i.e., the kinds of books available in high-quality children's bookshops) give children many positive answers to the long-term question "Why read?" Real books are fun and beautiful to look at; they arouse the emotions, which basals never do, and they provide fascinating information. And they're *really* entertaining—just as entertaining as television. They are the sorts of books that give birth to a desire to read, that engender lifelong reading habits rather than short-term agony.

We used to learn to write, too, in meaningless parts and bits, by filling in the blanks in ditto sheets with one or two words, or by answering inane questions about banal, vocabulary-controlled stories that tended to bore our teachers as much as they bored us. Ditto sheets were and still are unreal, pointless forms of written language. No one in real life fills in ditto sheets. Ditto sheets do not develop higher-order thinking, or an ability to write coherent, continuous prose, yet students have to fill them in for hour upon wasted hour throughout their education.

Unlike ditto sheets, real writing always conveys a real message from a real writer to a real reader, or readers; and the message is always one in which the writer has some kind of investment—in other words, *something hangs on the outcome.* Nothing hangs on the outcome of a ditto sheet, whether it's correctly filled in or not.

I rant and rave about "real" rather than "whole" language because real language isn't a vogue that can be discarded in years to come as just another passing fad. We use real language whenever we speak, write, read, or listen. We always have and we always will. We hear real sentences, with real meanings, in whole conversations. We read real paragraphs in whole books. We write whole words in real notes, real letters, real job applications, real advertisements, and real stories. We speak real sentences with whole messages. Whole language—in or out of school—is real language. It is my strongly held belief that reading and writing in schools should have the same reality as reading and writing out of school. If it isn't real we are wasting our students' time and stunting their language development. Unfortunately much of the language currently practiced in schools *is* unreal and *is* a shocking waste of time.

Happily there are already many schools in which children have been allowed to tap into the power of real language. On a recent visit to Sydney I found myself in a classroom literally humming with reality. Carina (not her real name), an angelic-looking but sexually abused child, had written and composed a song in my honor, inspired by many readings of *Koala Lou.* It had been entirely her own idea. A teacher had transcribed the tune so she and Carina could teach it to the class. A poster of the words hung on the wall. In the special visitors' chair I sat expectant, and waited.

Carina took up her baton and, pointing to the first line, steadied herself. The music started and the children sang such a sweet song about the absolute constancy of mother-love I wanted to lie on the floor and abandon myself to sobs. I did cry, openly, but managed to keep my wilder emotions under control for fear of alarming the children.

There were no ditto sheets or basal readers in Carina's classroom. Here endeth the lesson.

20

Only in America

I n June 1988, the Society for the Scientific Study of Sex (S.S.S.S.) was holding its annual convention at the Holiday Inn, Chicago, when I checked in. Intriguing conversations occurred between delegates in the lobby and in the elevator and waiting in line for a table at breakfast. In the same hotel, at the same time, the Lutheran Church of the Good Shepherd was also holding its annual convention, and I tried to imagine the reactions of each group should it wander mistakenly into a session being organized by the other.

It could only happen in America. Whenever I'm there

I'm constantly jolted into thinking, "Only in America!" It's an amazing place and I adore it.

In Florida, when I was there in that same northern summer of '88, an item of jewelry was being advertised on television, a medallion on a chain to be worn at all times in case one had a heart attack, epileptic fit, car crash, or any other sudden accident. The medallion proclaimed the wearer to be a Christian, thus alerting those who would rush to the rescue that prayers for the victim would a) be appropriate, and b) be likely to be answered, and that it was therefore probably worthwhile to send up a prayer or two on the wretch's behalf. The medallion was called a "Christian Alert Button." Only in America! I wondered what would happen to those not wearing a button in similar circumstances. I also wondered what God might have to say about not praying over non-Christians. My feeling was that He'd be pretty annoyed about it, and pretty upset, too, that Christians were being so miserly and discriminating about their Christian action.

I first went to America in late 1985 to attend an English teachers' conference. It had taken me thirty-nine years to pluck up the courage to step off a plane in that country, so sure was I of being raped, robbed, mugged, or murdered within minutes of arriving. When I relate this earlier fear to my American friends they're open-mouthed. Most have never witnessed or been involved in violence of any kind. In twelve visits in seven years I have yet to meet a person who owns a gun. I had thought that they all owned guns.

In New York once I had to take a cab from Columbia University to the American Express office on Lexington and Sixty-third, which meant driving through Harlem. I hoped the cab wouldn't break down. My imagination was alive to possibilities of violence and ruin since I'd just finished reading Tom Wolfe's *Bonfire of the Vanities* and still felt as if I were one of the characters enmeshed in the lives, corruption, and New York ugliness of that brilliant book.

I wasn't harmed in Harlem and I've traveled the subway in New York alone and often and without incident. I guess in a population of 250 million the proportion of violence per person nationwide is tiny. It's just that outside America we hear a lot about the crazies who murder on a whim or gun down half an elementary-school class in a fit of depression. These are the news items that jaundice our view and horrify our sensibilities, distorting the American reality and making us afraid.

Even at the age of thirty-nine I wouldn't have gone to America had it not been for James Gray, who set up the famous San Francisco Bay Area Writing Project. We met at a writing conference at the University of Norwich in England. He's a very round older man with large feet and brilliant ideas. I fell in love with him. (I'm always "falling in love" with men—and women—in a way that leaves Malcolm unmoved and unthreatened. "I mean," says Malcolm, "I don't know what you *see* in him!") When Jim discovered my physical fear of coming to America he threw up his hands in patriotic astonishment and, promising to look after me, urged me to visit. Two other American academics who were sitting with us in that dimly lit university pub also promised to lend a hand in my acclimatization.

So I went. And then I went back. And as my academic reputation blossomed, and more and more of my children's books were published there with the acclaim that one receives only in America, I kept on going back. I have fallen in love with the place, but I must never live there.

America is very bad for someone like me. My parents' values, which normally surround me like an iron wall, are scratched and sullied and chipped away in the U.S.A. (My mother still has a marked influence on my behavior. In one of her weekly letters in November 1989 she wrote, "I'm glad you spend a bit of time being grateful. There's a lot to be grateful for, with so much success and so many good friends and your happy home.") I'm concerned that in America I might shock my mother and myself by being tempted from my relatively ordinary life into a giddy world of fast lanes and questionable values.

My greatest fear, which isn't confined to America but is more pronounced in that country, is that of being molded by others into a person I don't recognize. I realize I wrote *Possum Magic,* and other books besides, but does that warrant the deferential admiration I experience as I move from Australian conferences to American colleges and back again via bookshops, schools, and libraries? Does being a successful writer make me a better person? More tolerant? More generous? More pleasant? I'm thrown into confusion by the attitude of readers and listeners who treat me as if I were wholly wonderful. I'm anxious because of the danger that at any moment I may come to believe I am indeed wholly wonderful. It's as if there were two Mem Foxes: me and the Other Mem Fox. I feel comfortable with the first, but very awkward with the second.

At home my family and students keep me in line. So do my friends: they're not impressed. They know me. All this Other-Mem-Fox stuff bores them and makes them impatient.

"Life's too short," says Rick.

"Cut it out, Foxy," says Lyn. "Be real."

In Australia I'm agitated by the fear of becoming a tall poppy and the subsequent pain of being cut down. In America, I notice, tall poppies are fertilized and encouraged to grow even taller, but I don't belong in America, and I don't really want to belong there. America encourages me to believe that I shouldn't be happy with what I have, since what I do not have could give me so much pleasure, especially if I were earning the minimum of a thousand dollars a day, which I have been assured could be mine for the asking—and sometimes is.

These temptations, when I analyze them in pages of fast writing in my journals, are easy to resist so long as I keep my head. The wealth I experience in that land of plenty is tremendously exciting, but nowhere in America do I find sufficient evidence to support the idea that wealth and happiness are synonymous. With this lie, however, television advertising mesmerizes its public, making into kings and queens those who own most, and own it most ostentatiously. Not that I would wish to be poor in America either, nor anywhere else for that matter. But in England and Australia in my experience people are more able to find contentment at a lower level of materialism, a contentment arising out of the solidity of families and friendships and a more happy-go-lucky attitude to life and work. In the U.S. work and ambition seem to have no ending.

The American work ethic is incredible even for me, and I'm not work-shy. Everything is urgent. Everything is a crisis. I arrive in Nashville, Tennessee, late at night, after a thirty-eight-hour flight from Australia via Los Angeles, Denver,

and Chicago, to be sat down at the airport for a 10:00 P.M.
business meeting about my tour schedule, which begins the
following day. My New York agent calls me early in the
morning in New Hampshire, where I'm working in a tiny
rural school, wanting this information and that by fax, by
yesterday.

On book tours I'm whisked from libraries to bookshops,
from schools to child-care centers, from people's houses to
public receptions, from university lectures to church halls,
my eyes glazed from the speed of movement and the lack of
sleep. My days begin at crack of dawn with social breakfasts
eaten in fast-food outlets, and end five engagements later at
10:30 P.M. So constant is the smiling that by the end of the
day my cheekbones ache. So constant is the being-on-my-
best-behavior that I take more time than is necessary whenever I go to the "john" just to relax and have a little peace,
quietly and all alone, counting to ten and breathing deeply.

The questions I'm asked are so similar as I travel around
the country that I wonder if I'm repeating answers people
have already heard. "I'm here for a month. I've been to
Vermont, Boston, and Chicago. I'm on my way to New York.
After that it's New Orleans, then Nashville, and after that
across to Florida, then over to California and home."

"I've never been West myself. You sure are seeing the
country, ma'am."

"I sure am."

Whenever I hear *ma'am* in the States it sounds so like
"Mem" that I look up, ready to say, "Yes?" and remember
just in time that no one in the Dallas airport is likely to
know who I am.

The minor cultural differences between America and

Australia are unsettling. It's like walking along a familiar road and being suddenly tripped up by a wire strung across my path. Bang! Down I go. For a start, Americans swear less badly and less frequently than their counterparts in Australia and England. Words that are mild in Australia produce shock-horror reactions in the States. Nice ladies say, "Oh, shoot!" instead of the other word. Once, when I was talking to a class about being a writer I told the kids that my first drafts were usually really "crappy" but that I didn't give a "damn" about it since I knew rewriting would improve them. As one, the entire class clapped its hands over its open mouths and, wide-eyed, turned around to watch the teacher's reaction. I blushed to the roots of my hair. If they'd known what I could have said, given a free rein!

Subtle changes in vocabulary are also surprisingly difficult to handle. I understand the meaning of American words, but having to say them myself at first made me feel as foreign as a non-English speaker. I was tentative, and lacking in confidence. The first time I was told, urgently of course, in an airport to "take a right" I was perplexed. I'd never heard the term before. Now I'm sufficiently familiar with it to be able to tell others to "take a left and walk a coupla blocks and you'll see it. . . ." The route to anywhere is called a "rout" and people don't live at the beach, they live by the ocean. Is the time twenty *of* seven, twenty *past* seven, or twenty *to* seven? It turns out to be the last. Unlike our "Happy Christmas!" theirs is never happy, it's always merry, and more often, so as not to exclude or offend non-Christians, it's not merry at all, it's "Have a happy holiday!" And they have a lot of "precipitation" rather than plain old rain.

Food and drink cause further confusions. When an air hostess asked me what I'd like to drink—"Wine? Soda?"—I didn't know that "soda" meant all soft drinks like Diet Coke, Pepsi, and lemonade. (And I didn't know that lemonade was Seven Up instead.) Tea is usually iced, and their biscuits are our scones, and our biscuits are their cookies.

In restaurants, waiters and waitresses greet guests with such a warm and pushy familiarity that I reel. And to think that once Malcolm thought Australians were too open and friendly! He'd find it an incredible affront to have a total stranger smile and say, "Hi! How're y'all doin'? My name's Courtney, and I'm your waitress this evening. If you wannannathing you just let me know, okay?" The entrée is not the entrée at all, it's the "main course," which comes in a wide and decadent number of choices, each of which is described down to the last detail of every ingredient by some Courtney or other with a phenomenal memory. Somewhere in this lengthy description there is usually an "erb" (they don't use the *h*) that they call "bayzil" and we call basil.

The choices of how to have one's coffee go way beyond the mere "Coffee or decaf?" to the point, at the end of a long list, where even decaffeinated espresso is a delightfully pointless option. If one finally chooses café latte there are still choices as to what to put on top of the froth: chocolate, cinnamon, or nutmeg.

The grammar is either excruciating or fascinating, depending on my mood at the time. I find it fascinating that we say, "How are you going?" when they say, "How are you doing?" But I must confess to an internal, high-pitched scream of horror whenever I hear the very common, "Oh, it was so fun!" and even worse, "Thank you much." Airline

201

staff all use the incorrect meaning of the word *momentarily*: "Ladies and gentlemen, we'll be deplaning momentarily" means in a minute, not, as I understand it to be, for a moment.

Americans don't stand in queues. Never in *queues*.

"You in line, lady?"

"Pardon?"

"You in line?"

"Oh, yes. Sorry. Sure, I'm in line."

No one says *sorry* either. That's a dead giveaway. Everyone says, "Excuse me" instead. So do I now. In America.

There are other, gentler differences that are charming, such as the little boy who showed me a handwritten story of his, pinned up on a classroom wall. Hands in his pockets, rocking back on his heels, he asked with pride, "So, Miz Farx, how do you like my penmanship?" One evening when I was out to dinner with my editor from Abingdon Press, in Nashville, the waiter came to refill her coffee and she put her hand over the top of it. "Ah don't care for any more, thank you," she said. So Southern-accented, so polite. So different from "No thanks."

At an American Library Association convention in New Orleans I offered to help pack up a book display at the end of the day and was told, "You cain't work, honey. You jus' gotta sit there 'n' look purty!" I thought they only talked like that in Hollywood musicals. Before I left someone asked me if I'd seen the author Jane Yolen that day and I heard myself go Southern and say, "Why no, I never did." In Australia I would have said, "No." And when I've arrived back in Australia exhausted, I've stunned the family by saying, "Ah'm jes' wore out. Ah'm jes' all done in."

In different states I've had a good time, a "real blast" in fact, and "geez Louise," this will "fracture you": I had breakfast with a friend who had maple syrup on her French toast with bacon and eggs. Isn't that "a stitch"? I've poured milk, from a "creamer," not a jug, into a "mean" cuppa coffee made by my host. When I lost a notebook on a plane and started looking for it a man said, "Did 'y'all' have writin' on it?" How could one of me be "all"?

American ignorance of things Australian has lessened as a result of the success of films like *Crocodile Dundee* and *Mad Max*, but I was rocked on two occasions to discover what people didn't know. A nice young woman studying for her master's in San Antonio, Texas, tried to tell me that Texas was bigger than Australia. She was furious when I told her gently that a map of Australia placed sideways on a map of the U.S.A. left very little showing underneath, but she cheered up when I told her that our total population was 16.5 million, about the same as the population of Los Angeles. Of course she thought Texas was big. Many Texans don't even leave Texas to go on holiday interstate. After all, "The sun is riz, the sun is set, and I ain't outta Texas yet."

Then there was the boy in California who asked what language we spoke in Australia. (This was in 1988.) I said, "The same language as the one they speak in England. England. Can you guess? Class? Anyone?" Eventually I had to tell them that in Australia—and England!—people spoke English. It made me wonder what was actually being taught in the schools in Texas and California.

Yet another difference between the English/Australian character and that of its American counterpart that I half love and half hate to watch is the making of phone calls in any airport. Whereas the English would hunch themselves around the phone, their backs to the madding crowd, practically whispering, desperately praying that no one will be able to hear a word they're saying, Americans do the exact opposite. Leaning outwards, facing the teeming mass of waiting passengers, they engage in private conversations in loud voices for all to hear, without a scrap of embarrassment. I'm the one who's embarrassed. Blushing on their behalf, I bury myself more deeply into the *Oscar and Lucinda* of the moment, hoping that the characters in the book will speak loudly enough to drown out the volume of these outrageous strangers. Only in America!

Yet I love it. I love the pulse, the energy, the vitality, and the pace of America. I love the expansiveness and kindness of Americans. I love the bagels in New York, the sourdough bread in San Francisco, and the coffee everywhere. I love the way they love my children's books so hugely and openly and I love my publishers in New York and Nashville, in Dartmouth and San Diego.

My books remain almost unchanged in their American editions. I insist on it. After all, we have to swallow American and English cultural differences all the time, so it's only right and proper that they should have to branch out and have an unadulterated taste of ours from time to time. Finding a publisher who would take *Possum Magic* unaltered took years. They wanted to change *lamingtons* to *brownies*, and *vegemite* to *peanut butter*. I stamped my foot. Better to remain unpublished, pure and untainted, I thought, than to cave in to this bullying cultural colonialism, particularly as I'd set out in the first place to write a quintessentially Australian book. In the end, a map of Australia and a glossary of terms were added at the back of the book to enlighten the ill informed. And I did allow *track* to be replaced by *path* in *Koala Lou* because of the railway-track connotation in America. In neither of those cases, however, did I feel that I was selling my cultural soul. I'll never do that. I feel too strongly about my identity as an *Australian* writer.

When I don my other hat in America, as a teacher of teachers of writing, I'm fortunate to be an Australian. We have taken the best of the excellence that New Zealand has to offer in the teaching of reading, added it to the exciting new theories and practices in the teaching of writing from the U.S.A., mulled over it, refined it, practiced it, matched it to the way children learn to talk at home using natural ("whole") language, and we've discovered in the process dynamic theories and practices of our own.

We've also discovered, startled, that we have become leaders in our own field. Our articles are read by doctoral students and published in journals in which Americans themselves would kill to be published. Stupefied, we travel to the States at the invitation of their experts, in order to spread the word. Dazed we stand, not knowing quite what to do or where to look, during standing ovations after our presentations.

It's heady stuff. How could I not love America? How can I not return like a yo-yo to that only-in-America admiration in spite of its extraordinary threat to the purity of my soul? As long as I keep running home to my unimpressed students and my pleased-to-see-me family in quiet little Adelaide I think I'll be all right.

In case I've given the false impression that every man, woman, and child in America knows who I am, I'll redress the balance with the child in Nashville, Tennessee, who listened to me speak for half an hour and then asked, "Are you from Tennessee, ma'am?"

"No, I'm from Australia," I said.

"Okay," he persisted, "so how come your name's 'Memphis'?"

21

The Kookaburra
and I

Why have I written an autobiography at forty-five, when it must remain, due to my comparative youth, incomplete?

The first reason is to alleviate the problem of Being an Object of Study. A huge increase in interest in writers and writing has meant that the mountain of mail that pushes itself into our house every week threatens to crush me under its weight unless I attend to it immediately. Students from kindergarten to Ph.D. level write from all over Australia and the United States, full of compliments—that's fine—but also bursting with questions that take hours to answer. Because of the letters-with-questions my correspondence can take up to eight hours a week, a wearying if flattering chunk of time to subtract from a full-time lecturing life. I'm tired. So *Dear Mem Fox* will lighten the burden of my correspondence by presenting, I hope, all the answers to the usual and unusual questions, thereby providing more time to respond with speedy pleasure to the sentences that don't end in a question mark.

My second reason for writing this book is one I've already mentioned, cancer. I wanted, in my obsessive way, to knock my life into a tidy shape, to pigeonhole it neatly, to tie it up into well-organized bundles, just in case the cancer fairy who beckoned once, beckons once again. Morbid though it may seem, my life is packed and I'm ready to go.

My third reason for breaking into this kind of writing was the desire to crawl out of the picture-book cage in which I'd hunched uncomfortably for years, to discover how it would feel to stand up and stretch in a book, unfettered by lack of space, freed from the gaze and requirements of my young audience. It's been a hazardous yet emotionally healing adventure, more fun than I'd expected, and often highly dangerous as I wandered off into hitherto unexplored territory.

So what's what then, in the here and now, at the end of this first half of my life? My husband is still Malcolm and we still put Christmas airfares ahead of more essential items on our list of priorities. We still argue about the division of labor in our house. And he still does not cook. In 1987 Malcolm was appointed to the staff at "my" college (now called The Flinders University of South Australia), where he lectures with flamboyance in drama and drama-in-education while I teach in the closely related world of language arts. Students who experience the two of us often speculate on what it must be like to live in our house.

Chloë is still talkative, still maddening, and still a perfect delight. She's almost twenty-one. She has graduated from university, and her heart is set on journalism, which does not surprise us at all. Our small nuclear family is rounded out by two terrific little terriers and a very grand cat.

My parents are still alive and still content in Africa. Lailu, my "baby" sister, lives in Adelaide, and Jan-the-brain is in London. There is much visiting between us all. Airfares assume importance in all our lives, not just Malcolm's and mine.

In between home and work my writing life still has its attractions, most of which manifest themselves away from my desk and pencils, since the act of producing readable writing is too grueling to be called an attraction. It's when I'm out and about that being a writer becomes a pleasure rather than an effort.

Once, for example, on a plane to Brisbane on my way to a conference, I happened to be wearing jeans, sneakers, and my *Possum Magic* sweatshirt. As I walked down the aisle to the toilets I noticed a woman staring at the *Possum Magic* design. On the way back to my seat she tapped me on the arm.

"That design comes from a book," she said loudly. "It's called *Possum Magic*." Other passengers turned their heads to look.

"I know," I murmured, red-faced. "I wrote it."

"You never!" she replied. My only means of identification was a driver's license with *Merrion* written all over it, so I returned to my seat with her suspicion warming my back.

On my passport I've listed my occupation as lecturer and writer. As I was leaving Australia for Zimbabwe in 1987 an official looked up and said, with bored skepticism, "Writer, eh?"

"Yes," I said, "writer."

He was unimpressed.

"What do you write?"

"Kids' books," I said. "For really little kids."

"Oh, yeah. Like what?"

"Like *Possum Magic,* for instance."

"Possum Magic?" Suddenly he was beaming. *"Possum Magic!* Top book! Me wife's brought it home for the bub."

Because I visit so many schools and tell stories on educational television, lots of the children in my neighborhood know who I am. When I meet them in the supermarket, they grin and stare, apparently surprised that I need to shop.

"Hi, Mem Fox!" they say. "Mum, that's Mem Fox, that one, over there." Blushing, I suddenly find much to interest me in the pet-food section. But I enjoy these brief encounters—they're usually fun and easy to cope with.

Once, however, I was attending to a complicated postal transaction when a boy, his older sister, and his mother came and stood at the counter. There's an assumption that people who are well known are blind and deaf, so the boy said without lowering his voice, "That's Mem Fox."

"No, it isn't," said the sister.

"Which one?" said the mother.

"That one," he said, pointing at me. They all stared.

"It *is* Mem Fox," said the boy.

"It is not," said the girl.

"I don't think it is," said the mother.

"It is," said the boy. "I know it is."

My burning face should have told them that the boy was right, but I could tell they weren't convinced. The sweet boy had my sympathies. While I waited for the correct stamps I scribbled a hasty note on a scrap of paper. It said, "You were right. It is me. Love, Mem Fox." As I left I walked past him, looking straight ahead, and with a rapid sideways movement of my arm reminiscent of Groucho Marx, I thrust the note into his hand and disappeared outside.

Schools are a delicious source of fun. After *Possum Magic* had been published, making me the proud author of one book, a small girl slipped her hand into mine and said, "Mrs. Mem Fox, you know what?"

"No, what?"

"I've got *all* your books at home!"

There are times when I forget that junior primary children don't always know the meaning of "Any questions?" Many of them understand it to be an invitation for personal news.

"Any questions?"

"My mum's had a new ba-by!"

"I'm having my birthday, not next Saturday, but the Saturday after."

"Our dog got runned over."

Noticing the rising alarm in the teacher's eyes I rephrase my question.

"Is there anything you'd like to know about writing books? . . . Yes?"

At last we have a question.

"How many acres have you got?" This is in a rural area.

"A quarter of an acre."

"A *quarter?*" Less than five thousand doesn't rate a mention. The questioner subsides, disappointed that my land holding is so deeply insignificant.

Finally one child asks, "How many copies are there of *Possum Magic?*"

"More copies than it would take to cover a football field," I reply.

"Oh, boy! How long did it take you to write them all out?"

Now we're warming up. The idea of questions about books and writing has caught hold of the class.

"How do you make the writing so black? Do you have to press hard?"

For the child, it's no laughing matter. The teacher and I dare not look at each other.

In one class, knowing that I was coming to visit, the teacher had been reading my books for weeks. There'd been some confusion over *Hattie and the Fox* having been written by Mem Fox. I was a person, not a fox, the teacher had explained. The morning before I arrived she'd asked her class who was coming the following day and was dismayed when there was no answer.

"Come on, kids, think! Whose books have we been reading?"

Eventually a tentative hand went up.

"Could it be Brer Fox?"

This hilarious and pitiful recompense for trying to be a great writer for kids hasn't deterred me. I still love visiting schools although the pressures of teaching and writing simultaneously mean there's less and less time to indulge in it.

The pace of my life leaves me ragged much of the time. In spite of the fact that I refuse seventy-five to a hundred requests annually to speak to a variety of audiences, I still manage to tie myself into knots of tension that cause a major collapse at least twice a year, during which I howl my eyes out and wonder how I've allowed myself to get into such a state yet again. At times like these I feel so trapped and desperate that I want to crouch in corners to ward off the blows of my frenzied existence. I long to run away, and wish I had no commitments. I even regret having written a single book and wonder how it would feel to be "normal." These low moments last only long enough for me to be forced to rest, take stock, recover, and leap into life again.

It's the unexpected that tends to throw me into despair, such as coughs and colds that turn into bronchitis and asthma, or the masses of marking at the end of each semester that turn my routine inside out, or the publicity engagements that mark the launch of each new book, squeezing themselves into the tight corners of my days. "Why don't you give up teaching?" people say, especially those who know that I currently earn far more from part-time writing than I do from full-time teaching. I couldn't bear to, that's why. I love it. And there's no way of giving up being a writer either, although sometimes I wish I could. The books can't be pulped, and the reputation can't be expunged.

Nevertheless, there are moments of relative stillness and calm in my life. Conversations with Chloë, for instance, keep me lounging around for hours as her childhood chat changes into lively adult companionship. And Malcolm and

I walk on the beach in all weathers every Saturday and Sunday afternoon. The same time. The same beach. The same walk. The same dawdling conversation, planning, laughing, remembering, sorting out, sharing, slowing down. And then there's time with friends at lunch, on the phone, at films, at dinner. My shoulders straighten, my clenched fists unlock, my forehead relaxes. I change into low gear and travel more safely for a while.

Right now my life is at the height of its summer and I'm reveling in it, grateful for its fruits. In the winter of my days, when these green memories lose their leaves and wither, I imagine I'll turn the pages of this book and marvel at my good fortune, wondering whether I exaggerated here and there since there's so much mention of sunshine and so little mention of rain. Outside my window, a kookaburra sits on an old gum tree laughing in the gathering dusk, celebrating with me, this high summer. The book is written. We're feeling on top of the world, the kookaburra and I.

Yet the story continues. The ending is not The End.